G. J. (George John) Whyte-Melville

Sarchedon

Vol. III

G. J. (George John) Whyte-Melville

Sarchedon
Vol. III

ISBN/EAN: 9783337173340

Printed in Europe, USA, Canada, Australia, Japan

Cover: Foto ©ninafisch / pixelio.de

More available books at **www.hansebooks.com**

SARCHEDON

A Legend of the Great Queen.

BY

G. J. WHYTE MELVILLE,

AUTHOR OF 'THE GLADIATORS,' 'HOLMBY HOUSE,' ETC.

IN THREE VOLUMES.

VOL. III.

LONDON:
CHAPMAN AND HALL, 193 PICCADILLY.
1871.

[*All rights reserved.*]

LONDON:
ROBSON AND SONS, PRINTERS, PANCRAS ROAD, N.W.

CONTENTS OF VOL. III.

Nisroch the Avenger.

CHAP.		PAGE
I.	A Serpent on a Rock	3
II.	Before the Altar	16
III.	The Snare of the Fowler	29
IV.	The Veiled Queen	44
V.	Aryas the Beautiful	56
VI.	A Wind from the South	69
VII.	The Fenced City	81
VIII.	Sons of the Sword	99
IX.	Faithful unto Death	111
X.	A Fool in his Folly	120
XI.	Bow and Spear	133
XII.	Lost and Won	146
XIII.	Sharing the Spoil	158
XIV.	Counting the Cost	171
XV.	The Voice of the Charmer	182
XVI.	Requited	196
XVII.	Betrayed	207
XVIII.	Who is on my Side?	218
XIX.	Forgiven	231
XX.	Lost in the Dark	243

NISROCH THE AVENGER.

'Your sin follows steadily behind, as the cart-wheel follows the draught-bullock.'
Bhuddhagosa Proverbs.

SARCHEDON.

CHAPTER I.

A SERPENT ON A ROCK.

A SOUTHERN sun beat fierce and pitiless on the terrace of the queen's palace at Babylon. Hewn out of the solid rock, a smooth and glistening pavement refracted those noon-day beams like burnished metal. Not a breath of wind arose to cool the heated air; not a bird dared spread its wing against the burning sky; yet Assarac stood motionless and thoughtful in the open unshaded space, heedless alike of throbbing brain, blistered skin, and sandals scorching under his very feet.

Suddenly he started and stepped quickly forward, like one about to trample something beneath his heel. Checking himself in the act, he paused to mark a serpent gliding along the unfriendly pavement, as if seeking for a hole or crevice wherein to shelter its shining skin and smooth, flat, cunning head.

He had thought to slay it; but no, it was not in him to do the creature harm, as he stood watching it with wistful eyes, and bitter thoughts, and a strange sad feeling of compassion at his heart.

Uncoiling many a sleek and glistening fold, it worked its way slowly, painfully, traversing in all its length and breadth the surface of that pitiless pavement, so different from the dank morass and tangled brake for which its nature yearned. The wise reptile, type of caution, intellect, sagacity, measured its cunning in vain against the beautiful impenetrable slab, could find no solace in the hard unyielding stone.

'Is it better, after all,' thought Assarac, 'to wind, like this wily creature, along the devious paths of policy, or to take the straight and open road, leading to danger indeed, but to danger that may be foreseen, assailed and vanquished with the strong hand? Would I be the tiger, blind with desire of blood, leaping at the wild-deer's throat, to slake a cruel thirst? or the serpent, crafty, patient, persevering, exhausting all its ingenuity, all its devices, against an obstacle smooth and impenetrable as this adamantine pavement, heated by the sun's rays, not to warm and cherish, but to scorch, wither, and consume?'

Thus meditating, with an unusual cloud of despondency on his brow, Assarac turned away, and traversing the large cool hall of the queen's palace, walked thoughtfully through leafy wilderness and shaded pleasure-ground to the silver temple of the Fish-God, where he had been summoned by Semiramis, that he might assist with his counsels the great design on which her heart was bent.

Kalmim, who had again resumed attendance in the household of her royal mistress, rejoicing that the days of mourning were at last expired, waited as usual in the porch.

With winning smiles and sparkling eyes—since Kalmim's bow was always bent for practice as for slaughter—she drew those silken hangings that screened the presence of Semiramis, and admitted him to the court of ivory and silver, as she had admitted Sarchedon once before, when that comely warrior arrived from the camp, bearing the signet of the Great King.

The queen had not forgotten. Something in the

gesture of her tirewoman, something in the murmur of doves, the babble of waters, the scene, the place, the listless noon-day heat, recalled that other interview but too forcibly now, and she received Assarac with a languid loving smile.

The eunuch's whole nature glowed beneath her glance, while, prostrating himself at her feet, he pressed the hem of her garment to his lips, with such rapture and devotion as he had never felt for Baal, Nisroch, Ashtaroth, nor all the host of heaven.

Her favourable looks emboldened him to speak; and after the formal salutation, 'Great Queen, live for ever!' he offered his advice unasked, in a burst of impassioned eloquence, very different from his usual composed immovable demeanour.

'It is a war,' said he, 'of which the new-born babe in the land of Shinar may never live to see the end, unless indeed it should terminate in an advance on Babylon by innumerable hosts, under the leadership of Aryas the Beautiful, and the sacking of our city by those swarms of fierce savages who congregate in the wind-swept deserts of the north. The Great Queen's arm reaches far, her hand is strong and skilful; but, trust me, she is about to plunge it in a very hornets' nest!'

'And crush them like locusts in my grasp!' exclaimed Semiramis, all her beauty kindling into flame, while she threw up her graceful head in feminine defiance. 'I make no war with drones, sparing their lives and taking away their gods, yet exacting small tribute of cattle or slaves; but when the insects carry stings, it is worth while to conquer and destroy. They breed *men*, I hear, beyond the Zagros range—men stronger and fiercer, like their own storms, the farther you march towards the north. I will carry back ten thousand of their champions, chained in pairs, to make sport for my fickle people here in Babylon. The blind fools! they are as proud of their queen's might as if it were their own. 'Twas a good stroke of yours, Assarac, that enabled me to resume my woman's garment at will. You welded the iron like a cunning smith while it glowed and sparkled on the forge. I could not patiently endure the constant restraint; I never should have guessed how irksome it is to be a man.'

'Irksome, indeed,' said the eunuch, 'so long as women have softer skins, stronger wills, and harder hearts. But the prince himself made the very opportunity that foiled him. I did but whisper in the Great Queen's ear to seize it. And though she drew her bow almost at a venture, the arrow flew deftly home, according to her wont.'

'Nevertheless,' answered Semiramis generously, 'it was *your* eye that aimed the shaft, though my finger pulled the string. I have always esteemed the head that counsels far above the arm that strikes. By the beak of Nisroch! I believe that I have not in the land of Shinar so wise and true a servant as this high-priest of Baal!'

For answer, he was fain to kiss the hem of her robe once more. When he tried to speak, the words seemed stifled in his throat. With one of her rapid glances, she even detected something like a tear glisten in his eye.

'It is far better and easier,' she continued, 'to reign for myself, and meet my people frankly without disguise. While I personated my son, I felt in every word, every gesture, the likelihood of detection; and they were beginning to hate me as a king. I saw it every hour. To hate without fearing—a fatal sentiment in such subjects as mine, whom I can govern easily as I can rein Merodach, but by far different means. The ruler of Babylon must have a frank brow, a close mouth, a sharp sword, a long arm, and an immovable heart. When I reigned here in the absence of the Great King, ere he—ere he—went before us to the stars—who can reproach me that I ever turned one step aside, for any consideration of pity or compunction? And yet, did you not hear, my friend, how they yelled and shouted, leaping for joy to think they had got their queen back again? Ah, they have not come to the end of it yet! And now counsel me, Assarac. What is to be done about the prince?'

'He is safely disposed,' answered the eunuch, keeping his eyes steadfastly off her face. 'Nevertheless there is no gate so close but it may be opened by treachery, no wall so high it cannot be surmounted with a ladder of gold. The captains of ten thousand are loyal and trusty warriors, yet who among them could resist a tempter offering the leadership of the host? I would bestow my lord Prince Ninyas in a prison from which no captive escapes, a fortress friend and foe are alike powerless to break through. There is yet a golden throne vacant in the sky, and he might take his place in it without delay, by the side of the Great King.'

It was a ghastly proposal; yet Semiramis seemed to listen without astonishment, and rather in sorrow than in any outburst of anger or dismay. She answered in a sad, thoughtful, and dejected tone:

'Such a measure would be wise, I grant, and would set the question at rest for ever. But I must not — I will not — consent! I cannot but think the doves that fed me in my infancy have imparted something of their nature to mine. I loved the boy dearly all his childhood through; none the less, perhaps, that in form and features he seemed so entirely mine own. I was a good mother to him, as any sun-burned peasant who brings her babe into the vineyard on her back; and, will you believe me, Assarac? he cared more for a rough word or a rude jest from the Great King than for my fondest caress, my smiles, my very tears. When I have pleaded with him, even to his own advantage, he has turned his back on me, and laughed outright.'

How strange it seemed that any man on earth could see that matchless face unmoved, hear that sweet voice unwon! But Assarac dared not speak, lest all his self-control should fail, and Semiramis proceeded with her complaint:

'He loved the meanest dancing-girl out of the market better than the mother to whom he owed his life, his beauty, his favour with the Great King. He would leave me for horse, and hawk, and hound, without a word — the ring of a timbrel, the flash of a torch, the clink of a wine-cup, would have taken him from beside my dying bed; and yet I cared for the lad through it all, sheltered him many a time from his father's anger, and screened his weakness, his incapacity, his vices, from the people over whom he thought some day to reign. I have done too much for Ninyas, and I have had no return. When I sent him to Ascalon with that white-faced girl, I thought we were rid of his follies for a space, to the profit of every one concerned. I never dreamed she would leave him, nor that the child loved its toy so well as to follow even to the gate of Babylon. That he should ride through in woman's attire must have been arranged expressly by the gods. Had he come in his own person, I had been compelled to act with less mercy. I thank you again, Assarac, that you saw the opportunity at a glance. One so sage in counsel, so quick in action, cannot but be skilful in war. Ere this year's dates have turned to russet, you and I will flaunt the banner of Ashur in the very face of the Beautiful King before his gate at distant Ardesh, and water our horses, whether he will or no, in the swift Araxes. War is the sport of kings, and am not I more king than queen when I mount my chariot in harness and headpiece, armed with bow and spear?'

'And does love count for nothing in the project?' asked the eunuch, with so much of reverence as masked, but did not quite conceal, a bitter sneer.

Semiramis turned from him in obvious displeasure: under the delicate ear he marked her very neck grow crimson with a blush. He bore pain well, this priest of a false god, and proceeded to urge his objections in the calm tone befitting one who offers counsel to a superior.

'Has the Great Queen counted well the cost?' said he. 'Has she considered how many bones of men and horses must whiten the line of march to rearward of her armies, ere they pass the Zagros range? Can her chariots of iron penetrate its wooded defiles? How shall her camels climb its steep and slippery rocks? Say she advances to the fertile country beyond the hills: she must either encounter those terrible savages, who worship a naked sword as the sons of Ashur worship Nisroch and Baal—gigantic warriors, clad in skins, but armed with bow and spear, eating human flesh and drinking horses' blood—or she will behold a barren plain before her, its peasants fled, its wells choked up, its harvest wasted by fire, affording neither food nor water to man or beast. When she has surmounted these obstacles, with the loss of half her strength, she will find herself face to face with a countless host of horsemen from the northern desert, under the leadership of Aryas the Beautiful himself.'

In many respects, she was a woman to the core.

'I have heard he *is* beautiful,' she answered with a light laugh.

His reply was grave and sad:

'Could not he have met Semiramis, at the frontiers of her empire, in all honour and splendour, without encounter of armies and shedding of blood? Must he, too, rue the youthful manhood and comely face that bring him a captive to the Great Queen's chariot-wheels, because of her ungovernable desire—'

'How, slave!' she burst out fiercely.

'For glory and warlike renown,' continued the eunuch; adding, humbly enough, 'My life is in her hand. Let the queen take it, here, at the shrine of Dagon, rather than do aught which shall prejudice her honour and her name.'

She looked appeased.

'It is mine honour,' said she, 'that this matter immediately concerns. I send an embassy, demanding a certain captive at the hand of Aryas; and what is his reply? Neither gifts nor tribute, nor words of homage and respect, but two winged arrows bound together by a link of gold. It needs not the dark wisdom of the Egyptian to interpret such a sign. He means that this is no question of barter or ransom, but one to be decided between us by bow and spear. It is the issue I most desired in my heart.'

'He means that the Comely King and the Comely Queen should join their hosts, and bind themselves together in a link that can never be dissolved,' murmured the eunuch, almost with a groan.

She smiled in beautiful scorn.

'I have the arrows in my quiver,' said she; 'the first shall be shot into his camp, the day I meet him face to face, with its feathers dipped in blood. It may warn him, perhaps, that I have sworn to drive the second with mine own hand through his heart. There are goodly men in the world, I trow, besides Aryas, and one ten thousand times as fair is wasting in captivity even now. Prate not to me, Assarac! I tell you, that if I wrap the world in flames, I will have Sarchedon back, here in Babylon, before this year's dates have fallen from the palm! I am sick till I see his noble face again. It is enough: I have spoken.'

Then the eunuch knew he was dismissed, and passed out of the temple sadly, thoughtfully, with drooping head, folded hands, and slow dejected step.

Crossing the terrace once more, he looked about for the serpent; but it was gone.

Calling to mind its struggles and windings, he wondered where and how it could have found rest, foiled at every turn by the glowing surface of that smooth unimpressionable stone.

CHAPTER II.

BEFORE THE ALTAR.

But for priest, as for warrior, there is no respite from daily duty, to be discharged with scrupulous care and unfailing zeal, however sore may be the heart within, aching under linen garment or proven harness of steel. Assarac must needs officiate at the altar of his god an hour before the sun went down, even had a victorious enemy been wasting the city with fire and sword, or had his own life been about to terminate with the first shadows of night.

How he loathed the mummery, that yet made him all he was; the machinery of which he knew so well each cog-wheel, catch, and lever; the false glare and sparkle that seemed so poor a substitute for the steady rays of truth! And yet he dared not whisper, even to his own heart, how mean and paltry was all this artifice by which he climbed to power.

He had a new religion now—that religion of the heart which sweeps wiser creeds away in a flood of blind unreasoning devotion; which degenerates, without a misgiving, into the wildest fanaticism, and can number its martyrs, as compared with those sacrificed to any other superstition, at the rate of a hundred to one.

He did not conceal from himself that he loved the queen—he, for whom the love of woman must ever be as the blind man's desire for light, fiercer, perhaps, and more ungovernable, because of the very impossibility that it should be realised. Cruel are the pangs of a hunger which is not even fed by hope. Intolerable is a thirst to which the very offer of water seems but mockery and aggravation. Nevertheless, he did not care to strive against his folly now. For a time, he had believed himself invulnerable — thought his very nature kept him safe—and that, for him at least, there must ever be an insuperable bar between admiration, regard, sympathy, and the slavish devotion which others called love. After admiration had become indiscriminating, regard unreasoning, and sympathy painful, he shut his eyes to the truth for about a day; but when he opened them, yielded without effort, plunging wildly into the abyss, owning a certain morbid pride, in the consciousness of his self-immolation, the while.

And now heart, brain, and faculties were all saturated with the poison. His strong will yielded gladly to the spell; his keen intellect was content to follow where it ought to lead; and had the queen bid him help her, as she said, to wrap the world in flames, his own hands would have brought the fire, though it scorched him to the bone.

To say that he loved is to say that he was jealous; but the torture he suffered was to that of other men as a cancer feeding on the vitals to a flesh-wound lacerating the skin. *They* might fret and struggle, gnashing their teeth, raving vengeance, threatening reprisals, alternately worsting the rival and reproaching the idol; but *he* must suffer in silence, smiling however sad, erect however crushed and humbled, outwardly serene though troubled to very madness within.

And all unvisited by a ray of light, a glimpse of hope, even by the dream of what *might* be, which has gilded so many a weary night-watch with fleeting visions of the dawn. Surely, through its very degradation, there was something sublime in such utter self-abasement, such complete self-sacrifice of love!

And yet his port was never more assured, his step firmer, his aspect more dignified, than when, after this interview with Semiramis, that had stung him to the core, he took his place at the altar to offer the usual evening sacrifice to his god.

The sun was sinking, and its level beams shed a crimson flush on the white garments of a band of priests, as on the spotless alabaster columns that crowned the lower story of the temple, supporting those upper chambers, of which the mysteries were veiled to eyes profane. A hundred steps, broken by five stately terraces, led down to an open space, in which thousands were crowded to witness the ceremony with upturned faces, that glowed no less vividly than did altar, shrine, and priests in the warm red lustre of a setting sun.

As in the morning to the east, so in the evening sacrifice the people turned themselves to the west.

A score of oxen stood lowing behind the altar. It seemed the poor beasts felt some forebodings of the fate that awaited them; though not till incense had been burned and drink-offerings poured out were their throats to be cut, at a given signal, and their flesh roasted for the consumption of that lavish god, whose daily service thus required the presence of a thousand satellites. These stood, marshalled like warriors, in rear of Assarac and Beladon, who assisted him in his functions. Swinging their censers, they continued chanting, or rather muttering, in a low voice and a minor key, certain formal repetitions, detailing the names and quality of their deity.

After a short delay, during which Assarac kept his eyes steadily fixed on the setting sun, he advanced before the altar, followed by Beladon, who waved above his superior's head the mystic ring, which, enclosing a representation of wings, formed the emblem of that incomprehensible power whose attributes were ubiquity and eternity. The eunuch's gait and gestures were solemn and imposing in the extreme; his ornaments of massive gold, his spotless robes, deeply embroidered, falling in heavy folds about his person, his fine stature and noble bearing —all were calculated to enhance his own dignity and that of the sacred office he fulfilled. Turning slowly to Beladon, he received at the hands of that assistant a golden cup filled with wine to the brim, and poured from it gravely a libation to the four quarters of heaven, finishing with the west. A hundred priests then advanced, chanting their hymns in time to a measured march, a hundred timbrels rang in sounding strains to the praise of Baal; and while fires were kindled, while smoke went up, and music swelled, the blood of twenty oxen flowed round the altar, filling the channels cut to receive it with a bubbling crimson stream.

Assarac and Beladon stood on each side, facing the people, wrapt, as it were, in a holy trance. Men looked on them in awe-struck wonder as votaries under the immediate influence of the god, whom Ashur himself, coming down from his throne, might address face to face, who were communing even now in spirit with the souls of departed heroes, with all the powers of all the host of heaven.

Little did they think how the eunuch's whole being was possessed at that very moment by a human vision of the brightest eye that ever shone in promise, the sweetest lips that ever kissed or smiled; while his attendant, yielding to desires yet more of earth, earthly, pierced the crowd with a gaze that, for all its semblance of holy preoccupation, did but seek a well-known female figure, alluring of form, lavishly attired, and not too closely veiled.

No sooner had the sun gone down, the stars come out, than Beladon, whose time was now his own, sought one of those courts which formed a communication between the temple of Baal and the king's palace, supposed by the people of Babylon to be occupied by Ninyas in a retirement from which their present temper would have rendered it extremely dangerous for him to emerge. Semiramis had returned to live in her own royal dwelling, where she held such state as caused all former magnificence to pale. The king's house, therefore, as it was called, became comparatively deserted; and with the exception of its wooded parks or paradises, fenced off for game, no spot in the whole city could have been so secluded as that in which Beladon lingered, pacing to and fro, stopping, muttering, glancing about him in fretful perturbation of spirit, peculiar to one waiting for a woman on whom he cannot quite depend. 'At last!' he exclaimed, catching sight of a veiled figure gliding amongst the arches that skirted the court, like a ghost in the dubious star-light. 'At last! And I saw you in the midst of the multitude before the sun went down, looking on at the sacrifices. Where have you lingered, woman? and what have you been doing since?'

Kalmim, for it was none other, raised her veil and laughed in his face.

'Who hunts learns cunning,' said she. 'Who

toils learns skill. Who waits learns patience. With cunning, skill, and patience, even a priest may come at what he desires.'

'Kalmim,' he exclaimed earnestly, 'do you believe there is nothing I would shrink from that you bade me undertake? Are you assured that I am constant and true as your own shadow on the wall? Do you trust me as I trust *you*?'

She had an object; and laid her hand on his arm with a pressure that implied a world of confidence, while she answered,

'Stanch as string to bow, hound to slot, a woman to her mirror, and a man to his desire. We have never been less than friends, Beladon, why should we? Perhaps, at last, we may be something more.'

He had an object too; therefore, resisting the impulse that prompted him to pass his arm round her waist without farther ceremony, he assumed an air of respectful devotion, and observed,

'I have no secrets from Kalmim; I trust her without reserve. There is not a question she could ask me I would hesitate to answer from my heart. Will she do as much for me in return?'

'Of course!' she burst out frankly, while her

bold black eyes looked him through and through. 'What do you desire to know?'

'Arbaces was my friend,' he replied abruptly. 'The Great King's chief captain fell shamefully murdered in his own dwelling. His daughter was carried off by force into the desert. What has become of her now?'

'You love her!' she exclaimed, turning her head away in feigned vexation. 'You love Ishtar, the cunning white-faced wanton! I ought to have known it; I *did* know it all along! And yet *you*, Beladon— I thought you so different from the others. O, it is hard to bear! How could I have been so weak? How can I be so foolish now?'

She had put him thoroughly in the wrong. Surprised, alarmed, perplexed, perhaps not a little softened and flattered, he hastened to excuse himself with more ardour than discretion.

'It is for Assarac,' he stammered, 'not for me. The chief priest saw her awhile ago in the market, and she has escaped him—*him* who can track a bird in the air surely as a camel on the sand! He bade me trace her. That is why I came to *you*.'

It passed through Kalmim's mind, that if Assarac set such store by the discovery of Ishtar's refuge, the information she had power to give would only be of value so long as it was withheld. If she would get her price, she must beware of submitting her merchandise to the light of day. The good-will of her customer too must obviously be secured in the first instance.

'And you do not love her yourself, Beladon?' she sobbed. 'You are sure of it—you will swear it—on—on—the altar of your god!'

The storm had lulled—yet not too suddenly. The heaving bosom, half-unveiled, though somewhat deep in colour, was not without its charms.

'By every altar of every god that reigns!' answered the deluded priest. 'By Ashtaroth, queen of love and light; by Baal, in whose very presence even now I stood; and by your own sweet self, whom I worship perhaps more fervently than all the host of heaven put together!'

'I cannot but believe you,' she answered, smiling sweetly, while she abandoned her hand to his caresses. 'Nay, it would make me very sad *not* to believe you, Beladon. Will you always be true to me?'

'Always!' he exclaimed, with an appearance of sincerity that might perhaps be attributed to his habit of making the same profession to every woman who was kind and fair.

She, too, was not without practice, and accepted the assurance calmly enough.

'You *do* love me,' she whispered, 'and, indeed, if ever I could bring myself to think of a priest, it should be one like—well, like Beladon, perhaps, though I sought in every temple through the land of Shinar till I found him. And now, if I tell you all I know, frankly and freely, will you promise me what I ask in return?'

'I promise,' said he, pressing her hand to his lips.

'Will you swear?' she asked.

'Can you not trust me without an oath?' he pleaded.

'Freely,' was her answer. 'But you must swear it nevertheless, to please *me*.'

'I *do* swear!' he exclaimed. 'By the Seven Stars —the Consulting Judges—the might of Baäl—the blood of Nisroch himself!'

'And by the three wings in the circle,' she added impressively.

He hesitated; but the dark eyes, softer and sadder than their wont, were looking straight into his own, the balmy breath was on his cheek. Kalmim had never before seemed so kind, so womanly, so lovable, and he committed himself to his promise by swearing that solemn oath which, neither in letter nor in spirit, did a son of Ashur ever dare to break.

She looked more than satisfied. 'I can tell you all about Ishtar,' said she, 'so long as she remained within the city walls, because I, who speak with you now, accompanied the girl, for old friendship's sake, beyond the southern gate, even to the Well of Palms, when she departed. She rode an old and sorry camel, bearing but a skin of water and a lump of dates. She was veiled and clothed for a long journey. I had nursed her on my knees when I was scarcely more than a babe myself; and I helped her, I own (for she is poor and lonely now), to beast, clothes, and provisions—though I begged hard of her to remain, little believing her earnest assurance, that if she could but find them, she had powerful friends in the wilderness. Nevertheless, even at the Well of Palms a tall rider had stopped to water his horse, and she did but speak a word in his ear, when he dropped on the sand to do obeisance at her feet. I was frightened, and fled to hide myself in the vineyards; but when I raised my head, they were riding away together into the desert with their faces towards the east. My own opinion is, that she has vanished from the earth like her mysterious mother, and gone back to the stars from which she traces her descent. And now, Beladon, that I have told you all I know, I claim from you the fulfilment of your promise and your oath.'

CHAPTER III.

THE SNARE OF THE FOWLER.

He had sworn by the eternal wings, and there was no escape. The wisest men in their dealings with women have pledged themselves, ere now, to give precious metal in exchange for dross, and Beladon made no better bargain when he matched his wits against the keener intellect and finer perceptions of the queen's tirewoman.

With grave aspect, and much decreased ardour, he answered somewhat ruefully:

'I will do your bidding—not only for mine oath's sake, but because of the love I bear you. Speak, then—your servant is waiting your commands.'

'It is not much I desire,' said she carelessly, though had there been more light he might have seen the blush rising to her brow. 'We women have strange fancies, you know; I would fain revisit my old haunts, and walk once more by night through the palace of the Great King.'

'Impossible!' he exclaimed, turning pale. 'You know not what you ask——'

'Impossible!' she repeated, mocking him. 'There is no such word acknowledged by the servants of Semiramis or Baal. Nothing is impossible, nor impenetrable, nor improper in the city of the Great Queen!'

'But my life would hang on your discretion,' urged Beladon, much disturbed—' on the silence of a woman, whose very office it is to repeat everything she hears, whether false or true!'

'And where could it hang more safely?' she retorted. 'Nay, Beladon, your welfare and mine are blended together like the bronze and gold of that buckle on your belt. The interest of one is the interest of both. Besides, think of your oath! Lead on.'

There seemed no help for it. Taking her by the hand, he guided her softly through those darkened courts and passages; urging, in impressive whispers, the necessity of secrecy, laying no light stress on the peril he was himself encountering for her sake. Thus gliding like shadows, they passed stealthily through the great hall of the king's palace, immediately beneath that *talar*, or upper chamber, into which Ninus had ascended when he poured his last drink-offering to the host of heaven, and was seen by his people here on earth no more.

She could not help shuddering while she recalled that awful night, when a great horror seemed to brood over the city, and men looked blankly in each others' faces, wondering what should befall them next.

Catching sight of the famous carbuncle over the gate, glowing, even in utter darkness, like a living coal, her fortitude gave way, and she screamed aloud.

However obtained, Beladon's experience seemed to have taught him that vigorous measures were judicious in cases of feminine alarm. Seizing her arm so impressively that she well-nigh screamed again for bodily pain, he whispered in her ear:

'It is death for both of us if we are discovered by the priests of Baal, who now guard the palace. I know my brethren, Kalmim, and I *love* you. Listen! I wear a knife at my girdle, and you shall die first!'

Thoroughly frightened, she hung her head, and held her breath. Could this be the free-spoken lighthearted Beladon, whom she had hitherto esteemed a mere frivolous idler, fit only to fill a place in the showy pageants of his god? He was rising rapidly in her good opinion, while in her characteristic love of excitement a certain thrill of pleasure sweetened the terror that admonished her how many risks she ran at every step.

Traversing the great hall, they emerged on a terrace commanding one of those pleasure-grounds for which Babylon was then no less famous than in after years for the celebrated hanging-gardens that adorned the age of her decay. It was a wilderness of shrubs and flowers, of grove and rock and stream—fit haunt for the game with which it had been plentifully stocked—fit retreat for luxurious royalty during the heat of an Assyrian day—fit hiding-place to secrete the fair favourite of a jealous lord — fit stronghold to immure the person of an imprisoned king.

Its recesses were distinctly visible from the terrace twenty feet above, on which Kalmim stood. At that elevation she looked over its entire length and breadth, while a bright moon, high in the heavens, flooded every nook and corner of this paradise with a light like day.

It was now dead of night, the wild bird had gone to roost, the wild deer was couched in its lair, yet a dark object moved across the lawn, on which Kalmim's eyes were fixed, slowly, stealthily, with long-continued pauses, like some feline creature prowling for its prey.

'Come away,' whispered Beladon in her ear. 'You have traversed the palace; you have seen the king's garden. It is time to depart.'

She made no answer. Her eyes were fixed and shining; her face set like that of a sleep-walker, or of one horror-stricken in a dream.

The figure turned slowly round. Its garments fell disordered and awry, its hair was dishevelled, its mien wild and scared, but none could mistake the beauty of that pale startled face; and in the miserable object thus stealing, shivering through the moonlight, Kalmim did not fail to recognise the person of Ninyas the king.

Surrounded by a dense column of spearmen, on whom threats, protestations, and remonstrances were alike wasted, the hapless son of Ninus and Semiramis had no sooner entered the city of his inheritance, in ill-advised disguise, than he found himself a helpless prisoner under the very eyes of his assembled people, shouting enthusiastic welcome of his return. So wisely had Assarac's measures been taken, so skilfully had he disposed the large force at his command, that

Ninyas and his attendant, spite of their struggles, found themselves engulfed, as it were, and swept away in a resistless rush of spears. Their horses' bridles were seized, the animals themselves urged to a gallop, the guards who hemmed them in drowned with noisy cheers even the acclamations of an excited populace; and so the whirlwind swept on unchecked towards the king's palace, where all Babylon was persuaded its beloved queen had betaken herself, there to assume the royal diadem and sceptre, ere she sought her own dwelling on the other side of the river.

But Ninyas shuddered while they hurried him under the outspread wings of those colossal bulls; for something told him they guarded a prison-gate, obdurate and impenetrable as the very granite from which their huge proportions were hewn.

'It is all over,' he whispered to Sethos. 'The bow is broke and there are no more arrows in the quiver. This is one of the Great Queen's masterstrokes. I ought not to have trusted her, and yet I thought my mother loved me too well to have worsted me like this!' Whereto his follower, from whose smooth and easy nature fortune, good or bad, glided without making much impression, only answered, 'A silken cushion is a softer couch than the desert sand; a palace in Babylon is a nobler lodging than the fortress of Ascalon. Baal himself knows not what the coming hour may bring, but the three wings never cease to turn their everlasting wheel, and the spoke that is lowest one moment comes uppermost the next!'

The cup-bearer's philosophy was so far borne out, that the royal prisoner found no reason to complain of his personal treatment. His banquets were sumptuous, his pleasures magnificent, his retinue submissive, as if he were in truth a king; but, turn which way he would, he encountered the smooth faces and downcast looks of the priests of Baal, who answered his questions with irritating professions of ignorance, and waited on him with a subservience maddening in its vigilant humility. To those whose very existence depended on the favour of Assarac had been confided the care of this important captive, and scrupulously they fulfilled their trust. Though he wandered at will from court to court and hall to hall of the roomy palace—though he might take the air, when it pleased him, in its gardens, or follow the chase in its wilderness—he knew that never for a moment was he unwatched—felt that words, looks, gestures, all were noted and reported, that his very thoughts were known; for while many of his wishes seemed anticipated, his attempts at escape were foiled almost before contrived.

This constant supervision could not but tell on such a nature as that of Ninyas, could not but injure a constitution already sapped by luxury and indulgence. His health gave way; his mind became affected. He drank wine indeed, freely, but neither ate nor slept, wandering listlessly to and fro, chiefly in the open air, regardless of times and season—during the hours of darkness, as under the glare of noon. Had it not been for Sethos, who attended him with touching fidelity, his intellects must have wholly succumbed, and perhaps the purpose of his incarceration would have been accomplished. But the cup-bearer exhausted all his ingenuity to rouse and keep alive the faculties of his lord, desponding, nevertheless, more than was natural to his cheerful spirit and tendency in all things to hope the best.

Kalmim, watching the king with sudden frightened gaze, marked how pale he had grown and wan, how shrunken seemed his stature, how loose the costly garments hung on his limbs.

Could he see her? She knew not. He started

indeed, and stood at gaze like a frightened deer, then muttered and ran on, looking up at the moon, pausing after a few steps, with drooping head and downcast eyes, to stare on the ground beneath his feet.

She was a hard, bold, pleasure-loving woman, yet her heart melted within her, and she wept.

'Are you satisfied?' whispered Beladon, in accents of considerable alarm. 'I tell you, it is death to know our secrets, death to look on the sight you now see. Will you not depart ere it be too late?'

But Kalmim, it is scarce necessary to observe, had another object besides that of an idle visit to the king's palace, in thus cajoling her admirer and risking discovery by the dissolute priests of Baal. She had reason to believe that Sethos shared the captivity of his lord, and with Sethos she resolved to speak, if such an interview could be brought about by woman's wit, woman's duplicity, or woman's charms. Laying her hand caressingly on his arm, she shot one of her sweetest glances in Beladon's face, and whispered,

'Be patient with me, if you love me. I do but ask that you will take me hence to the cedar gallery. I know my way then to the outer court, and so can depart in peace.'

Her quick wits reflected, that as a communication existed between the lawn and the cedar gallery, Sethos would be there in attendance on his lord.

The young priest pondered in some perplexity. It was his turn to watch all night over the seclusion of this important prisoner, and he had counted on the society of Kalmim to beguile the tedious hours till daybreak; but the risk of discovery by his comrades was too great, the penalty they would surely exact too hideous, and, for her sake, he thought better of his enterprise, even at the last.

'You do with me what you will,' he said, after a pause, in which she almost believed she could hear her heart beat. 'If I let you go free now, you will promise to steal softly out, silent as the dead. Whatsoever you see you will forget; whomsoever you meet you will pass unnoticed. All that takes place here must be as a vision of the night, to vanish with dawn of day. Swear it, by the Serpent of Ashtaroth!'

'By the Serpent of Ashtaroth!' she repeated, glad to escape on such good terms; and, true to her easy careless nature, added in a whisper that sent Beladon well-pleased to his watch, 'I am not ungrateful, as you know; when shall I see you again?—to-morrow, by the temple of Dagon, at noon?'

Nevertheless, her cheek paled and her breath came quick while she stole through the cedar gallery, because, light and fickle as she was, she *did* entertain for the cup-bearer something of that mysterious preference which makes a woman instinctively conscious of *his* presence whom she thus distinguishes from the rest of mankind; and, though she could not see five paces before her, she felt that Sethos was there, and would accost her as she passed.

He could be vigilant enough for the safety of his lord, and, if he was indeed slumbering, her light step brought him to his feet at a bound. The next moment she was in his arms, with her head on his shoulder.

'I have risked everything to see you!' she sobbed wildly; 'life, and more than life. O, Sethos, you are a prisoner to those who know not mercy, suffering none to escape. Do they use you well?'

His composure was sadly disturbed. It was startling enough to be accosted in the dead of night by this beautiful vision, glowing and panting in his embrace; but yet more surprising, surely, to find himself an object of such interest to the queen's tirewoman.

It is but justice to say that his first thought was for the safety of his unexpected visitor.

'How came you here, Kalmim?' he exclaimed, 'and how are you to get away again? Know you not that we are closely guarded by the priests of Baal? If they found you in their precincts, all the wings of Nisroch would scarcely save you from their wrath.'

'I am not so bad a captain,' said she, hanging fondly to his arm, 'but that I have secured my retreat. I made Beladon guide me to this spot. I know the secret passage hence to the outer court. It is guarded by a hundred of the neophytes, hewers of wood and drawers of water for the temple. They would as soon dare question Semiramis herself as the favourite tirewoman of the Great Queen. It is of *you* I am thinking, Sethos. It was to find *you* I came here at dead of night—to see *you*, to comfort *you*, and to consult upon some plan for *your* escape.'

The moon shone faintly into the gallery. By its light she could observe how sad was his brow while he answered, pointing to the terrace:

'Kings on their thrones have armies at command,

and hosts are left them after hosts have melted away. But this king in a prison hath but one subject to do his bidding. Shall not that servant stick closer than a brother, cherishing for his master a love surpassing the love of women?'

'It is impossible to save you both,' said she despondingly.

'Then save the king,' he answered simply and with a cheerful smile.

'Nay, Sethos,' said she; 'I would peril much for your sake, because—because—you never asked of me anything for yourself, and what you bestow on man or woman is given freely and without an afterthought. But Ninyas is one, and you are another. If I am to risk life and limb, it must be for the cup-bearer, not for the king. I am not like an armour of defence, to be put on or laid aside at will. Steel headpiece and linked habergeon ward off death from this man as from that; but, trust me, there is some difference between a harness of proof and a woman's heart.'

He looked kindly in her face, and a thought seemed to strike him.

'Even here, in our imprisonment,' said he, 'there sometimes reaches us an echo, faint and feeble, of rumours that stir the outer world. Is it true the

Great Queen has summoned an innumerable host to march forthwith on this expedition to the North?'

'It *is* true,' said Kalmim; 'and she leaves me here at home—*me*, without whom awhile ago she could not lay a plait not plant a bodkin. But that you are here in captivity, Sethos, and I shall be near you, it would have angered me bitterly, and I had reproached her roundly to her face. But let her beware! A smouldering flame is not a fire extinguished; and none was ever yet the better for offending Kalmim, with or without a cause.'

'In the queen's absence, there must be a governor of the city,' he whispered. 'Will the obedience of the people be given to such a one when their ruler is many a day's march away? O Kalmim, if Ninyas be ever righted, ever sit on the throne of Ashur in the palace of his fathers, I, even I, shall stand in a dress of honour at his right hand; and who but Kalmim will then really sway the sceptre, far and wide, over the whole land of Shinar?'

Her eyes flashed, her cheek glowed. No woman is so empty, so frivolous, but that she willingly entertains a project of ambition; and the last watch of night had passed away, dawn was already glimmering on the horizon of the desert, while Sethos and his visitor were yet taking earnest counsel together how they might restore the dynasty to its rightful heir, and sap, till it crumbled into ruins, the glory and power of her who was now supreme mistress of the eastern world.

CHAPTER IV.

THE VEILED QUEEN.

In all her reflected splendour as the wife of the great conqueror—in her richest lustre of youthful beauty—in her noblest state of royal magnificence while she administered for an absent husband the affairs of his boundless empire—never did Semiramis appear so glorious, so beautiful, or so queenly, as when she passed in review, on the frontiers of the land of Shinar, the innumerable forces she had collected, less, indeed, to gratify the cravings of ambition than of a softer yet more engrossing sentiment, which in her woman's heart predominated over desire of conquest and love of war.

Even with her untold resources, unscrupulous strength of will, and unquestioned power, it was no light task for the Great Queen to muster such a host as might invade the strange and distant regions for which it was destined, if not with certainty of victory, at least, without prospect of defeat. To the haughty Assyrian, polished and luxurious, though fierce and warlike, that rude inhospitable country, from which he was fenced by his northern mountains, seemed awful as the land beyond the grave. For him, the word 'Armenia' meant a place of horror, mystery, and romance. With Egypt he was familiar as with the sandy desert that parted him from his ancient enemy. Of Ethiopia, notwithstanding its scorching suns and endless wastes, he had formed his own ideas, sufficiently extravagant, attributing to its burning clime many demons, monsters, and other prodigies, yet wholly satisfied that all the powers of the south, in or out of nature, were as nothing before the face of Baal and the might of Ashur. The warlike Philistine tribes, even the redoubtable children of Anak, he had fought against, with varying success, gradually absorbing them in his own dominion or pushing them farther into the wilderness. It was his custom to conquer wherever he found room to drive his chariots and wheel his horsemen; but he had never yet penetrated beyond the Zagros range to the snowy peaks, the shaggy woods, the dreary wilds of the North. That he should meet with peril and adventure such as the veterans of Ninus had not even dreamed, he was fully persuaded; that he should overcome all obstacles, he had been no son of Ashur had he not implicitly believed; but that he was engaged in a formidable undertaking, and would encounter a powerful foe, seemed obvious from the enormous levies collected, and the gigantic preparations made to carry out the war.

The whole expedition was commanded to assemble within a few days' march of the frontier, there to receive final orders, and pass in review under the eyes of the Great Queen.

Wearing a dazzling harness of steel inlaid with gold, and a burnished helmet, on which blazed a ruby of such size and splendour that its rays seemed to play round her head like a plume of fire, Semiramis, standing in a war-chariot, revealed to her assembled hosts a beauty brighter than the metal, richer and more lustrous than the gem. Close by her wheel, so that she could mount him at a moment's notice, was led Merodach, caparisoned with crimson and gold. Not a warrior in the host who looked on him but swore that white horse with his eyes of fire was well worthy to carry so precious a burden. She seemed to prize him dearly, laying her hand on his smooth and swelling neck in frequent caresses, which the horse acknowledged with arching crest, brightened eye, and quivering ear, looking about him, nevertheless, as if not wholly satisfied, and neighing loudly on occasion when a burst of martial music, or the tramp of an armed column, seemed to wake in him certain memories of the heart, so faithful and so touching in that creation man is pleased to call the brute. Though Semiramis had broke him to her hand, and tamed him to her will, she could not teach the horse to forget his rider. Perhaps she loved him none the less that ear and eye seemed always on the watch for his absent lord.

Hanging diagonally against the panel of her chariot, within ready reach of her royal hand, swung a quiver of sandal-wood, containing but the two arrows which the Comely King had sent in answer to her haughty demand. She had sworn by Ashtaroth never to draw bow till she came face to face with Aryas, and then to return him his own warlike tokens in deadly quittance, accompanied each with five hundred thousand men.

Flashing back the light from its polished surface like a mirror of steel, the queen's shield, all chased and embossed with gold, was suspended at the back of her chariot. As the coveted office remained unfilled, every mighty man of war in the host had in turn believed he would be selected to bear it before her in battle; but Semiramis, having long since made her choice, kept her own counsel, determining to face the weapons of her enemies unfenced until she had set *him* free to protect her person, who was never out of her thoughts; who had obtained, perhaps from his very indifference, so strange an ascendency over her wild and wilful heart.

Assarac the eunuch, well pleased to accompany the expedition, coveted more than others this honourable post. When captain after captain had been passed over, a sweet intoxicating hope bade the priest's brain swim, and so changed his character that in a transport of enthusiasm he could forget alike the exigencies of policy and the dictates of common sense.

Descending from his chariot, he approached the position Semiramis had taken up, while the flower of her armies passed by in countless thousands, and, making his obeisance, proffered a request that he might be permitted to guard her safely with his life, in terms of the humblest devotion ever offered by a subject to a queen.

She laughed in his face — a kind frank hearty laugh, that stung him to the quick.

'What are you thinking of,' said she, 'my trusty sage and counsellor? Surely that weight of steel on your brow has disordered the workings of your keen and subtle brain. Know you not, that when Semiramis mounts her war-chariot, she drives in the fore-front of the battle? I tell you, man, I have had shafts and javelins flying round me thick as locusts on a field of barley in the blade! I have seen the stoutest captains of Ashur cower beneath that deadly hail! What would a priest of Baal do in such a storm?'

He was deeply hurt, and showed it. Had not he, the priest, the eunuch, confronted dangers in her interests at home to which the reddest battle-field that ever ran with blood was but a game of play? He felt within him a spirit of fierce and reckless daring far above the animal courage of the spearman, but he only answered sadly,

'I could at least die at the feet of my queen, making of my body a pedestal for her to crush and trample, if it raised her but an inch!'

With a cruelty, the more pitiless that it seemed so utterly unconscious, she turned on him her soft alluring glance, her sweet bewildering smile. Perhaps, because of his very nature, she was more lavish of such endearments to *him* than to others; perhaps, in sheer wantonness of beauty, she cared not what they were, nor how many, whom she scorched to death with the fire she thus flung carelessly about; but the avowed regard, the frank kindness with which she treated her devoted servant, were at once the provocatives and the punishment of his presumption.

Meanwhile he, the counsellor, the reader of the stars, the man of statecraft, of wisdom, the priest, the eunuch, was blindly, madly, in love with his queen!

'Could I spare you?' said she earnestly, even tenderly. 'Where should stand the pedestal from which Semiramis may look over a conquered world, but on the far-sighted wisdom, the unshaken fidelity of her best and truest servant? I tell you, Assarac, that you and I, beardless though we be, have more skill of war than all the captains of all this marching host; that rather than lose your counsel, I would send the half of mine armies, bows, spears, and auxiliaries, back to the homes they quitted at my command. And yet look on them, priest. By the beauty of Ashtaroth, these are not men to be despised!'

While she spoke, the chariots of Assyria were filing past her, two by two. Each, drawn by its three horses, contained its complement of warriors—its heavily armed bowman, his charioteer, and shield-bearer, all of whom were on occasion formidable foot-soldiers, strong, fierce, and skilled in the use of deadly weapons. In their midst waved the scarlet-and-gold banner of Ashur, representing Merodach, god of war, standing on a bull, with a drawn bow in his hand. Their appointments, their discipline, their very looks seemed to insure victory. The queen's eye sparkled, and the colour rose in her delicate cheek.

''Tis a gallant show!' she murmured; 'each comelier than his comrade, and every captain of ten thousand fit to mate a queen. Is it worth while to hazard all for one so little different from the rest? Yes; I hold that man was made for woman's pleasure, to destroy him how and when she will!'

The eunuch, hearing her last sentence, smiled sadly. 'So be it!' he answered. 'The altar must have its victim and the flame its fuel, but the votary is none the less destroyed that he is consumed in sacred fire.'

She heeded him not. The war-chariots had passed on, and all her faculties were concentrated on a troop of mounted auxiliaries, small indeed in number, but of gigantic stature, riding on horses strong, swift, and terrible as the desert wind with which they were accustomed to compete. 'What have we here?' exclaimed Semiramis, holding her bow above her head, and thus bringing the whole array to a halt. 'Have the winged bulls of Ashur come down from their pedestals to march into Armenia? Are these riders men or giants? Were their horses bred on earthly plains or are they born from the fire and the simoon? Behold! Surely they are led by a woman! As I live by bread, another warrior-queen! but veiled and shrouded like a housewife in Babylon, stealing out at night to the feast of Dagon. Halt them, I say! And, Assarac, command her hither to my chariot-wheels forthwith!'

The eunuch made haste to obey, and the small column formed line at once, facing Semiramis, man and beast quivering with repressed strength and spirit, held in subjection by the habit of warlike discipline. Their veiled leader took her place in the centre, sitting her horse tranquil and immovable as a statue.

A tall well-armed warrior rode out, however, from the ranks, and dismounting, prostrated himself before the queen, while his horse, waiting for him, watched his motions like a dog. Rising erect, it did not escape the notice of Semiramis, that his lofty head was on a level with her shoulder, as she stood above him in the war-chariot.

'Whence come ye?' asked the queen, 'and wherefore are ye ranged under the banner of Ashur, commanded by a woman like myself?'

'Thy servants are children of Anak,' answered the leader. 'They are free as the wild ass of the desert, paying tribute and owning subjection to none. They came out of the wilderness at the summons of the Great Queen, neither for gold nor spoil, but by *her* bidding whom their prophets foretold, a daughter of the stars, who has come down to lead her chosen tribe into the North.'

'Doubtless, from her seat on high she could see far and wide,' replied Semiramis with grave irony; 'and she has made no idle choice. By the beard of Nimrod, I have never set eyes on such men! And she, that veiled woman on the black horse, is your captain, then? How are ye assured she is indeed a daughter of the stars?'

'By the light in her eyes,' said he simply. 'Once before she appeared among us, and we knew her not, but suffered her to depart in peace, according to the prophecy—nevertheless, when she came a second time, the fire-god cleared our sight, and we beheld in her face the glory of those whom earthly mothers bore on the mountains to the sons of heaven. Our fathers looked for her in vain; but she has descended for us, their sons; therefore at her behest have we gathered under the banner of Ashur, in the service of the Great Queen.'

'Trust me, you shall not be idle!' exclaimed Semiramis; adding, with some curiosity, 'And this queen of yours? Is she then always thus shrouded and invisible?'

'It is death to look on her face,' answered the son of Anak. 'When she unveils before the enemy, behold, he will be consumed and waste away like water spilt on the sand. May the queen live for ever!'

Semiramis scarce concealed a smile.

'It is well,' said she graciously, making him a sign to retire. 'When the time comes, I doubt not you will quit you like men! Like men!' she repeated, turning to the eunuch; 'rather like the giants of our fathers' time, whom ye equal in size and strength. Surely, Assarac, we may take the Comely

King by the beard with warriors like these—tall as camels, strong as wild bulls, fierce as lions, foolish as the ostrich, true slaves of Ashtaroth, veiled or unveiled, eager to ride to death at the wave of a woman's hand!'

He looked wistfully after the stalwart forms, sitting their horses so proudly, as they trampled on in a cloud of dust; and his heart swelled with bitter sadness while he asked himself, which of these lusty champions would pour out his life for her so freely, so gladly as he, the eunuch, the priest. Must he always be tongue-tied? Would he never have courage to tell her? Could she not guess it, see it, feel it? O, if she knew! If she only knew!

CHAPTER V.

ARYAS THE BEAUTIFUL.

THOSE personal advantages of strength and beauty which caused the captivity of Sarchedon in a distant land served also to obtain for him royal notice and approval when he arrived at the place of his destination. The merchant who had purchased him from the Anakim knew well the price commanded by such specimens of manhood in an open market; but he was also aware of the fictitious value the king of Armenia attached to men of goodly stature and comely looks, who were skilled in exercises of war. This wily trader laughed in his beard while he reflected on the excellent bargain he had made with these simple children of the desert, from whose tents he led away his Assyrian purchase towards the mountains of the north.

Sarchedon, notwithstanding anxiety for the fate

of Ishtar, and sad forebodings of an endless banishment from his own country, had become so habituated to reverses that they affected his appearance and bearing but little; while, in spite of mental uneasiness, health and strength could not but increase under the care of the kindly merchant and his companions, journeying easily on, with frequent halts, breathing night and day the free open air, keener and purer as they neared those wooded mountains that formed a natural defence for the frontier of the Armenian king.

The trader, whose avocations led him to visit different countries bordering on the land of Shinar, spoke fluently the dialects of all. Springing from a common root, the language differed so little from his own, that Sarchedon mastered without difficulty such idioms and address as became an Armenian slave in presence of his lord. When, therefore, he reached at length the rushing waters of swift Araxis, and beheld the towers of Ardesh against the clear pure northern sky, he was fit, thought the trader, in every quality of mind and body to stand in a dress of honour before Aryas the Beautiful himself.

Ushered into the presence of the Armenian monarch, Sarchedon, lifting his eyes to take note of his future master, actually started to behold a form and figure that seemed, as it were, the reflection of his own in some magic mirror, glorifying and enhancing every quality for which he was himself most conspicuous. He beheld a man of similar stature, frame, and countenance; but the stature was a trifle loftier, the frame even more shapely, more graceful; while over the comely face, with all its kingly dignity, played a light smile, so feminine in its softness that it might well have irradiated the beauty of a twin-sister of Sarchedon.

To outward splendour of jewels and apparel the king owed nothing. His garments were of the coarsest texture and the simplest shape, such as became a hunter of the mountains who would have every limb free and unfettered for the chase. The bow in his hand, though tough, well-seasoned, and of formidable length, was rudely tipped with elk-horn, the sharp straight sword on his thigh hung in a frayed leathern scabbard, the sandals on his feet were of untanned hide, and one of them was stained with blood.

Yet Sarchedon gazed on him with an admiration he was unable to control. He had seen Ninus in pride and pomp of warlike power, Pharaoh dazzling in the blaze of his golden throne. The one, without his chariots and banners, might have been a mere war-worn spearman, the other, denuded of priceless gems and shining raiment, a peasant or a slave; but this man, standing unadorned, save by his comely face and noble bearing, looked every inch a king.

Twice he prostrated himself in unconscious and involuntary homage, and twice Aryas the Beautiful smiled on him well pleased; for he too could not but acknowledge the noble bearing and fair exterior of this stately captive, vowing in his own mind, that if the courage and intelligence of the Assyrian were in any proportion to his good looks, he would promote him without delay to the most honourable post in his court, that of bow-bearer to the king on all dangerous expeditions, whether in warfare or the chase.

As time rolled on, there sprung up a strange feeling of regard and attachment between these two men, so alike in person, so different in all besides. Such a feeling as is indeed rarely reciprocal when race, religion, and station are wholly at variance, when one is a monarch, the other a captive, one master, the other slave. Nevertheless, Aryas took no small pleasure in the society of Sarchedon, and the Assyrian entertained in return for this foreign prince a sentiment of loyal fidelity that bade him ignore hardship or danger, and count life as a thing of little cost in the service of his lord.

These feelings, the result of gratitude for kindly courtesy and gentle usage, grew to utter and entire devotion, from an event that took place soon after Sarchedon had been appointed bow-bearer to the Armenian king.

With all its feminine beauty of expression, the face of Aryas was that of a brave resolute man, well suited to such an athletic and graceful frame, as enabled the comely monarch to excel in bodily exercises demanding strength, agility, or endurance. He was passionately fond of the chase, and followed out his favourite pastime with a persistency and reckless daring that rendered it more laborious, and even more dangerous, than actual war. The Armenian lion, bred among the glens and fastnesses of those colder regions, was doubtless inferior in size and ferocity to his African brother, or even to that which Ninus loved to hunt on the sunny plains of the country between the rivers; yet was he a formidable antagonist to one who went out to meet him on equal terms, discarding the advantage of horse or chariot, but advancing on foot to take his enemy by the beard, opposing teeth and talons only with sword and shield. Such was the practice of Aryas the Beautiful, and Sarchedon could not control a transport of generous admiration when he witnessed the confident courage with which this royal Armenian slew the lord of the forest in single combat, rousing him to spring rampant against his buckler, and stabbing the mighty beast from beneath that defence, with well-directed thrusts of a broad two-edged sword, in ts tawny sinewy chest.

They were together in a deep ravine of that chain of mountains where tradition declared the first ship to have rested with its various cargo and its God-fearing crew, when the raven flitted round it to and fro, when the white bird of peace came back with an olive-branch in her mouth, ere she left it for evermore. Crowned by the dark and silent forest, the gray rock rose precipitous on either side. The king's retinue remained with their horses at a distance, and Aryas followed his prey into the defile, attended only by Sarchedon in his capacity of bow-bearer. It did not increase the Assyrian's confidence to know that his quiver was empty and his bow strained. Had Aryas been overpowered, he could have rendered him no assistance; and the horsemen must have gone round many furlongs ere they could have ridden down the mountain-side into this deep and dangerous gorge. Nevertheless, Aryas the Beautiful, with the bright smile and jaunty step of a peasant-girl going to market, tracked the lion's foot-prints one by one till he came up with him; and when the formidable game turned at bay, observed calmly to his follower:

'You are strong, Sarchedon, and I will help you; but 'tis a weighty carcass for you and me to carry up that steep when we have slain him. Nevertheless, I must have his skin at any cost. I want it for a foot-cloth in my war-chariot.'

Ere he spoke again, the lion was quivering in its death-pangs at their feet, and the king had drunk his fill from a clear cold mountain-spring, sparkling like a diamond on a cushion in its mossy velvet nest. With no little labour they carried the dead monster to their companions; and then for the first time it occurred to Aryas that the life of his attendant would have been somewhat wantonly risked if he had lost his own.

'Up in these mountains,' he said kindly, 'we are no longer lord and servant, but true comrades and brother hunters of the wood. That is why I love to come here. But we all take our share of sport and danger alike. Wherefore did you not tell me you were unarmed? Had my foot slipped on that strip of turf, you would have found yourself in no maiden's embrace, my friend; and stout as you are, yonder, I think, lies a better wrestler than you.'

'It was for his servant to follow where my lord led,' answered Sarchedon modestly; adding, with the inborn pride of his nation, 'The sons of Ashur are little given to fear; but if a man lacked courage, he might borrow all he needed from such an example as is afforded by my lord the king.'

'Nay, my friend,' replied Aryas, laughing, 'I have no such superfluity to lavish, for I see my danger clearly when I confront it. Nevertheless, where there is no fear there is no courage, as there can be no fortitude where there is no pain. But I will not suffer my followers to risk life for my amusement; and when we reach the dark forest you see yonder across the valley, to drive the mountain-bull from his covert and chase him over the plain, you shall be as well armed and mounted as myself.'

By such frank dealings with his inferiors, such kindly consideration for others, the Comely King had so attached his attendants to his person, that it was generally believed amongst his subjects he possessed some magic amulet compelling all that came about his person to love him and do his bidding. Perhaps they were not far wrong, and the charm he used had in it much of strange and subtle power; for men cannot resist a fair face, a frank manner, above all, the kindly sympathy of a brave and generous heart.

Leaping on his horse, the king bade Sarchedon change his bow, replenish his quiver, and follow him across the defile. As he plunged down the steep after his leader, over slabs of rock affording but slippery foothold, and through broken ground clothed with tangled brushwood, Sarchedon found himself wishing more than once for the sagacious instinct and obedient paces of his own Merodach. The animal he rode was strong, active, and full of mettle. For all common purposes he could not have desired a better; but when a man is galloping at speed over unforeseen obstacles, where a false step is a certain downfall, he learns to appreciate that electric sympathy, the result of constant companionship, which constitutes so subtle and mysterious a link between the horse and his rider. Merodach would obey an inflection of the body readily as a turn of the rein, would spring to the gentlest pressure as to the lustiest shout; but Merodach stood picketed far off under a southern sky, and Sarchedon's horse was on his head twice ere he rose the opposite hill to come up with his leader, who had halted for a few moments that he might look about him and observe his ground.

'We have the wind of them,' said Aryas, pointing to a few indistinct dun-coloured objects glancing like shadows in and out amongst the trees. 'But they are disturbed, and have left off feeding. When their heads are up like that, they mean moving, and pretty quickly too. Dost see that broad-leafed oak standing by itself there over the waterfall? Gallop round it, man, without drawing rein, and you will be in the thick of them. They will not expect danger from that quarter, and even if they do make a rush for it, you will turn the old bulls to me.'

While Sarchedon obeyed, the Armenian king unwound the scanty fold of linen that formed his head-dress, and permitted it to float at length on the breeze, thus distracting the attention of the wild cattle, now thoroughly on the alert, from their enemy.

Sarchedon galloped on unnoticed so long as his horse's footfall was lost in the roar of the torrent. When within a bow-shot, however, the herd became aware of his approach, and forming line almost like the horsemen of Assyria, paused for a space while they roused themselves to fury, throwing the earth about them with horn and hoof.

For once the king's wood craft was at fault. Preferring, as it seemed, a known to an unknown danger, they elected to bear down on the advancing horseman rather than make farther acquaintance with that long mysterious strip of white which had hitherto engrossed their attention.

Sarchedon now found himself called on to sustain the charge of the whole infuriated mass. While he fitted an arrow to his bowstring, his horse snorted and trembled, its eye turning blue with terror. He could but hope to discharge one shaft at the foremost, and then take his chance with the spear.

'The fool!' muttered Aryas, sitting like a statue, though eagerly on the watch, 'not to keep on their flanks. It was my fault,' he added; 'I should have warned him.'

Then he shook his horse's bridle and charged down at speed amongst the herd.

In the mean time the entire mass, headed by the oldest and heaviest bulls, came thundering on against Sarchedon. Their leader he transfixed, indeed, with an arrow through its mighty neck; but the animal, with a roar of rage and pain, only lowered its head and made at him with the more fury. Had he been on Merodach, he might have escaped; for watching its attack with wary eye, he would have evaded the collision, and stabbed it as it passed by; but the horse beneath him had now become unmanageable from fright, would answer neither heel nor bridle, and, turning its flank towards the enemy, was rolled up by the wild bull in a confused mass, with its prostrate helpless rider.

Looking wildly out from under his horse, Sarchedon saw the conqueror's eye glow like a living coal, felt its warm slaver streak his own defenceless face, and knew that ringed, curved, massive horn, brandished aloft with sidelong menace, would only descend to be buried in his entrails. Already the bitterness of death seemed past, when a horse's head showed over the wild bull's massive shoulder, an arm was raised to strike, and the ponderous brute went down almost across Sarchedon's feet, with spine and marrow deftly cloven by one lightning stroke from the sharp hunting blade of the Comely King.

Extricating himself from his fallen horse, the Assyrian bowed his forehead to the ground, and kissed his preserver's feet.

'My life is as a prey,' said he, 'delivered into the hand of my lord the king, who has saved it at the peril of his own. Therefore, in storm and sunshine, peace and war, good and evil, I am his slave for evermore.'

Aryas was measuring the dead bull's horn with his bowstring.

'I can get slaves enough for gold,' he answered carelessly. 'When I venture life, it is to buy a *friend.*'

Sarchedon's voice came very low and hoarse, and in his eyes shone the unaccustomed glitter of tears, while he replied,

'When I fail my lord, may my steed fall, may my bowstring rot, may my javelin splinter, and may the woman I love betray me to another for a measure of barley or a paltry handful of gold!'

CHAPTER VI.

A WIND FROM THE SOUTH.

DAY after day the friendship of these congenial spirits grew closer and more familiar. The Assyrian had related his own eventful history to his new lord, and Aryas seemed never weary of listening to the tale. Bold, enterprising, and imaginative, he loved to hear of the conquests of Ninus, the prowess of the sons of Ashur, the splendour of Babylon, the wealth of Egypt, and the many adventures through which Sarchedon had passed in his long journey from the tents of the Anakim to the mountain fastnesses of his own northern kingdom. He would inquire minutely concerning the evolutions and tactics of the Assyrian armies, the number of their chariots, the strength of their cavalry, the weapons of their men of war, and the proportion in which they made use of sling, bow, and spear; but he could not be brought to take any interest, apart from her warlike skill, in the character of Semiramis, paying little attention to the other's glowing description of her lavish state and luxurious magnificence, least of all caring to hear of her beauty, her attractions, the glory of her apparel, the lustre of her personal charms.

Even when Sarchedon poured his heart out freely on the subject of his beloved Ishtar, the Comely King listened, indeed, with a certain show of kindly interest, as due to the emotion of his friend, but obviously failed to appreciate the importance of the subject, or to comprehend the enthusiasm which could thus set up a pair of soft eyes and a fair face for the aim of a man's whole energies, the reward of his perils and his toils. He did not understand how a woman's smile could possess such attraction as the bray of a clarion, the flaunt of a banner, or the managed leap of a horse.

Beautiful exceedingly, formed to be the delight of the other, as he was the admired of his own, sex, love to the Comely King seemed but a foolish riddle, not worth the trouble of solving, an irksome study interfering with the pleasures of the chase, unmanly, untoward, but, above all, tedious and out of place when other affairs were on hand.

'Show me a woman,' said he, smiling at his bow-bearer's rhapsodies, 'with an eye like my falcon and a heart like my dog; so will I too drink myself drunk with this folly as with wine, to get sober again as surely, if not so soon. Till then, give me horse and hound, bow and spear. I tell you, Sarchedon, the whitest arm that was ever thrown round a man's neck could not yield me such a thrill of triumph and rapture as the lion's claw that tore me from loin to shoulder over my buckler while I stabbed him to the heart with my short sword, ere we carried him, you and I, up the mountain-side, and skinned his tawny carcase under the old oak-tree!'

Sarchedon sighed.

'I love the chase well,' said he, 'and warfare better, and Ishtar best of all.'

'Warfare!' repeated Aryas, catching and kindling at the word like a war-horse at ring of steel; 'talk to me of that till sundown, if you will! Ay, war is something to live for, something to die for, something on which to wage sceptre and kingdom and all, if only the foe be worthy of the venture. Could I but see the sons of Ashur drawn out fairly before me in battle array, I would fall willingly in their midst, and hold my fame was crowned since I had lived to measure swords with the conquerors of the South. But what do I say? These are dreams and unreal visions. Too many ranges of impassable mountains, too many leagues of scorching desert, lie between the gaudy pinnacles of Babylon and my rude towers here in Ardesh. I have not power to go to *him;* and I think, with all his courage, all his lust of conquest, the fierce Assyrian dare not come to *me!*"

They had spent the morning since sunrise in the chase, and had been so successful as to regain the palace in Ardesh by noon. After a rough but plentiful repast, the king and his bow-bearer were sitting over the embers of a brazier, each with an untasted cup of wine beside him, conversing as above. Scores of warriors and retainers, shaggy, tall, athletic, clothed in furs and skins, crowded round a huge wood fire in the outer court under the open sky; for although the sun was fierce and powerful, a storm of sleet had lately swept across the heavens, and these hardy champions laughed while they wrung their beards to dash the frozen drops away. There was a shade of despondency on the young king's brow, and he shook his comely head, while he reflected on the remote position of his kingdom, and suggested the impossibility of an Assyrian invasion.

Sarchedon started to his feet and listened.

'It is the tramp of a horse at speed,' said he. 'For good or for evil, there comes a messenger bringing tidings in hot haste to my lord the king.'

Even while he spoke, a stir in the outer court denoted some unusual excitement, while the fire was deserted for the gate, where a crowd had already gathered round a travel-worn horseman, dismounting from his reeking beast, panting and jaded with fatigue.

Sarchedon's face fell, and there was at least as much of self-reproach as of gratitude in his tone while he exclaimed:

'Cursed be my day, and oh! that I had never been born! Something tells me I have brought evil to the hand that fed and the roof that sheltered me. I know too surely that the enemy is at the gate, that the sons of Ashur are bending their bows against the safety of my lord the king.'

Aryas smiled, and his eyes glittered like a hawk's.

'Bring in the messenger,' said he in calm sonorous accents; adding in a lower tone to his bow-bearer, 'When, in return for fair words, costly gifts, and a dishonourable demand, I sent two arrows to the land of Shinar, the one a headless shaft, the other barbed and pointed, it was a token that Armenia, though desirous of peace, would never shrink from war. Had a dog sought my protection, he should have been safe behind a nation of horsemen. Shall I deliver up my *friend* at the whim of a proud lascivious woman, though she be twenty times a queen?'

'Alas,' replied the other, 'my lord knows not the might of Semiramis. She is immovable by pity, she is insensible to fear. All the hosts of heaven could not turn her purpose, nor thwart her desire. I will be the bearer of an embassy speaking words of peace from my lord the king. I will go back to put my neck under her foot, and abide my doom.'

'Let her come and take you!' was the gallant answer. 'By the sword we worship, she shall find the task a hard one!—ay, if for every bodkin she looses from her head-gear she can set in array a hundred thousand men!'

The messenger, a rude and hardy horseman of the north, had now arrived in the king's presence. Prostrating himself but once, and with scanty ceremony, he stood erect to deliver his tidings in frank bluff tones.

'I have ridden night and day from the southern frontier,' said he. 'Thiras the governor sends greeting to the king. He bids me tell him the south wind has brought up a flight of locusts, that darken heaven and cover earth with their swarms. Shall I speak yet farther in the ears of the people who throng the gate?'

Aryas shot one glance of intelligence at Sarchedon.

'Say on,' he exclaimed; 'I have no secrets from those who sit at meat with me in the city, and stand beside me in the field.'

Thus adjured, the messenger proceeded:

'The sons of Ashur have come up in their might from the land between the rivers. Their war-chariots shake the mountain as they pass, their horses drink the streams dry where they ride through. Thiras cannot count their numbers, and what could he do but offer earth and water for tribute, seeing that they muster under the banner of the Great Queen?'

Aryas started as if he were stung. The comely face flushed dark red, and rarely as he lost his self-command, some outburst of anger would surely have followed, but that another messenger arrived on the heels of his predecessor, if possible more hurried, more jaded, more travel-worn than the first.

He, too, scarcely prostrated himself in the royal

presence, and through the shaggy locks which fell across his brow his eyes shone with the terror of some wild forest creature hunted by the wolves.

'From Sambates, governor of Beznun,' he stammered, 'to the king greeting. They have cast a bank against Betlis, they have surrounded the great lake, and called it by the name of their queen. They have overrun the province, taking fenced cities, burning villages, laying waste corn-land and vineyard, slaying men, and carrying into captivity women and children. They are swifter than the south wind that brings them, fiercer than leopards, more terrible than the lightning, and numberless as the stars of heaven. What could Sambates do but offer earth and water for tribute, seeing that they muster under the banner of the Great Queen?'

Once again Aryas winced and coloured, but controlled himself the more effectually for the emergency of the situation. In the same instant he realised his peril, resolved to meet it, and calculated his powers of resistance. His first aim was to inspire his followers with confidence. Filling his scarcely-tasted goblet to the brim, he advanced to the outer court, and standing in their midst, bade them follow his example, while he drank the national pledge—

'To the Men of the Mountain and the Sons of the Naked Sword!' Then, taking his bow from Sarchedon, he broke it across, and cast the fragments at his feet in token that war was declared, while he thus addressed them:

'The wolves of the wood came up against the mountain-bull, and thought to slay him, saying, We are fierce and daring, my brothers, because we live on blood; and this creature cannot resist us, for his food cometh up under the dews of heaven, and he slakes his thirst in the murmuring stream of the hills. Also, we outnumber him a hundred to one. Therefore will we encircle him, and leap on him, and pull him down; so shall we fatten on his carcase, and drain the warm life-blood from his throat. Let us go up against him without fear, in an open space, rejoicing that he has been delivered unto us for a prey.

But a herd of wild deer were feeding in the plain, and when the wolves approached they took to flight; so the mountain-bull, grazing far above them, raised his head, and was aware of his enemy crowding and circling towards him, like the waves of the Northern Sea. Then he withdrew into a thicket, where he set his back against the solid rock; and when the wolves made at him, fiercely, but one by one, they dashed themselves to pieces in vain against his shaggy front, writhing under his feet, falling pierced and mangled by his mighty horns.

Men of the Mountain and Sons of the Naked Sword, is not Armenia strong and tameless as the wild bull of her hills? Are not the sons of Ashur innumerable and pitiless as the wolves that scour the forest, leaving only bones white and bare where they have passed? Ye have learned by these messengers that our country has been entered and our honour assailed. The banner of Assyria is flaunting in Armenian breezes, the sons of the Mighty Hunter are trooping in by thousands from the south, to slay and ravage and destroy. Therefore I call on you at my need, therefore I bid you to council; not to deliberate on a question of peace or war, for the bow is already broken and the sword unsheathed, but to advise with your king and leader how best we shall rid us of our enemy, and drive the wolf back, cowed, mangled, halting, and howling, to his den!'

Wilder, fiercer, louder with every peal, rose the shouts that greeted the Comely King's harangue, while he paused and looked about him, stately and graceful, like a master-stag at bay. Brawny arms were tossed, and naked swords brandished aloft in very ecstasy of warlike defiance, nor, of all those manly russet-bearded faces, was there one that failed to express intense hatred of the stranger, implicit trust and confidence in the might of Armenia, with a fixed resolve to die, if need be, at worst, fighting hard to the very end.

When the council which Aryas had summoned took their places for deliberation, there seemed but one opinion—that, gathering all their forces without delay, they should pour down into the plain, like their own rivers in flood, and, overwhelming the foe in their onslaught, sweep him back to the place from whence he came. Who could stand before the hosts of the North? Were they not Men of the Mountain and Sons of the Naked Sword?

It was the king's bow-bearer whose skill and experience tempered this bold resolve with a degree of caution, resulting from his own knowledge of the Assyrians' warlike resources. When it came to his turn to speak, though somewhat mistrusting his advice as an alien, none could gainsay the soundness of his argument, agreeing as it did with the half-expressed opinion of the Comely King.

Insisting strenuously on the countless numbers

of the enemy, and their overpowering strength in chariots and horsemen, he urged that it would be the height of imprudence to meet them in the open plain, where they would too surely be encircled and crushed by their enemy in a resistless girdle of steel.

'The wild bull,' said he, 'in the words of my lord the king, hath his rock, and the Men of the Mountain have their fastnesses. The wolves of the wood may dash themselves to pieces against the one, and the sons of Ashur spend their might in vain against the other. Let them advance here to meet us in the heart of Armenia, and so, falling on them weary, impoverished, and exhausted, let us fight a decisive battle under the very walls of Ardesh, and so destroy them, once for all, never to bend a bow nor lift a spear again.'

After much discussion, the stranger's advice was allowed to be sound and good. It was resolved, therefore, that the Armenian forces should be concentrated in the very centre of the kingdom, there to await the attack of Semiramis with her innumerable hosts; and the same decision seeming also good when discussed, according to Armenian custom, over the wine-cup, every man went home to sharpen his sword and fit his bowstring for the coming fray.

CHAPTER VII.

THE FENCED CITY.

'The storm has broke at last,' said Aryas, stooping to lift a headless arrow that had fallen at his feet. 'If it hail no deadlier missiles than this, there will be little glory in sheltering under buckler and headpiece, behind stone buttress and unbroken wall.'

Sarchedon took the arrow from the king's hand.

'Behold,' said he, 'the feathers are dipped in blood. Such a token is the deadliest of all defiance from my countrymen. My lord the king hath ever measured glory by danger. Trust me, he will have enough of both who holds a fenced city against which the armies of Assyria come up to cast a bank.'

'So be it,' was the dauntless answer. 'The god of our nation hath never failed us yet, and those can scarce refuse to accept the award of battle who worship no other power but that of the naked sword!'

They were standing on the wall of Ardesh, scanning anxiously the lines of the Assyrian camp, which now encircled them. The Comely King had here concentrated all his forces, and the hosts of Semiramis, disappointed, it may be, that they met so little resistance on their march, completely invested the capital of Armenia, where the men of the north had taken their stand, determined to put forth all their strength in a single blow, and finish the struggle once for all.

The Assyrians had surrounded the city by night. At dawn their trumpets sounded about it on all sides, and ere noon the siege had so far commenced, that the headless arrow, formerly dispatched to the Great Queen as a token from Aryas, was shot into his stronghold, to alight at his very feet, wet and stained with blood.

'She is here in person,' observed Sarchedon in a low grave voice, while he turned the arrow round and round in his hand. 'None of her servants would have dared to send such a messenger as this. It means war to the death, no ransom for the captive, no mercy for the wounded, no burial for the slain.'

'Is she, then, so pitiless a conqueror?' asked the Comely King, repressing certain hideous misgivings, that he had undertaken a task beyond his strength, and that not only his own life, which he was always willing enough to wage freely, but the safety of his people and the very existence of his kingdom were in the utmost peril.

'Merciless!' repeated Sarchedon. 'An eagle has mercy when she turns from the dead carrion, a lion has mercy when he is gorged; but how shall men look for mercy from the solid impenetrable rock? That woman has, indeed, the lion's courage and the eagle's ken; but her heart is stone. And yet she is so beautiful,—so beautiful,' he added, while a tide of wild and thrilling memories imparted a mournful tone to his revilings; 'I have seen a poor wretch she has condemned turn on her his last look, full of love and worship, ere they covered his face and led him forth to die. Is she not more than woman? Is she not Ashtaroth, Queen of Light, come down to lead the sons of Ashur to their doom?'

The king was straining his eyes towards the camp of the enemy. He cared as little for the beauty of Ashtaroth as of Semiramis.

'If she is with her armies in person,' said he, 'and leads the attack, I will slay her with mine own hand. Behold, when I have cut the string, her captains and men of war shall bend the bow in vain. Look out yonder, Sarchedon, over the eastern slope. You know the array of your countrymen in camp or line of battle. Surely where the chariots of iron are massed, down yonder by the waterside, between the lines of horses, should be the abiding-place of the Great Queen.'

From the rampart whereon they stood, a bluff face of rock descended precipitously towards the camp of the Assyrians. Such, indeed, was the defence of Ardesh on every side; the natural difficulties of the stronghold being enhanced by a solid wall of masonry, against which, even after a bank had been raised by the besiegers to the necessary height, their battering-rams might be plied for a considerable period without effect. Save on the eastern quarter, the fall was nearly perpendicular, affording no encouraging prospect to an attacking force; but here the cliff sloped off in an incline, up and down which a goat might travel freely, or an active man unencumbered with armour might pass to and fro. If Ardesh were to be carried by assault, this was its only practicable point, although the inequalities of the surface were so trifling, and the angle so imperceptible, that the ascent looked perfectly smooth and upright from below.

Leaning over, with his attention riveted on the camp of the enemy, the king let his helmet fall from his head at this very spot. It rolled several cubits down the incline, till caught by a projecting corner of rock, where it hung bright and glittering, like a morning dew-drop on a dead autumn leaf. Aryas looked after it and laughed.

'Token for token,' said he. 'A headless helmet in answer to a headless shaft. If it ever gets down to their camp, they may summon their wise men to read the riddle in vain.'

'It must not remain *there!*' answered Sarchedon. 'The flash of steel will draw every eye in the host to the only joint in our harness; and I know their cunning of warfare well. Let my lord the king shelter for a space beneath the wall, lest I draw on him a storm from yonder dark cloud of archers in the vineyard when I show myself. We shall have no more headless·arrows shot into Ardesh to-day.'

'I would I had known in time!' muttered Aryas. 'Not a leaf had been left on the vines to screen a marksman, not a hand's breadth of green but had been scathed and shrivelled by fire within a bow-shot of the walls. Well climbed, Sarchedon! By the sword of my father, the Assyrian hath a leap and footfall like a goat!'

While he spoke, the royal bow-bearer crept cautiously down the precipice, taking advantage of every inequality that afforded foothold, of every tuft and fibre of vegetation that he could grasp. Slinging the recovered helmet round his neck with a bow-string, and thus leaving both hands at liberty for his ascent, he returned even less laboriously than he departed; and surmounting the wall, stood by the king's side, panting, breathless, but exulting with boyish glee in the achievement of his exploit.

'And they marked me not from below!' said he triumphantly; 'though I dared not often trust myself to look down, I could have seen if bow had been bent or arrow pointed from the camp. Surely the Assyrian sleeps on his post; surely they have lost their discipline since I carried a spear in the guards of the Great King!'

'We will give them a lesson in warfare ere long,' answered Aryas, but though his tone was bold enough, his eye wandered uneasily over the mighty array of tents and banners that covered the plain below. 'We can hold them at our pleasure till the snow winds come to help us from the north, unless they give the assault at this very spot beneath our feet, and here, too, we are guarded by the river, shallow though it be; for if to-day it steals smoothly and gladly through the water-flowers, like a youth wooing a maiden to the dance, to-morrow it comes roaring down in a seething flood, unbridled and irresistible as a host of northern horsemen with a broken enemy in their front.'

But the king's prevision and the keen eyes of his bow-bearer were alike at fault. Thus it fell out that the only assailable point in the defences of Ardesh was laid open to an enemy who never failed to strike home without delay at the weakest place.

It had been the custom of the Great Queen, during their long and toilsome progress from the country between the rivers to the mountain regions of Armenia, to inspect with her own eyes the camp-life of her armies, and to satisfy herself of their nourishment, their comfort, their general efficiency, above all, their loyalty to her person and fidelity to the standard under which they marched.

For this purpose she would assume the disguise of a simple archer, hiding her face, as if to screen it from the sun, with the folds of a linen head-dress, such as has always been affected by inhabitants of hot climates, and so, often without a single attendant, would stroll unrecognised through the camp, listening to the rude talk of the spearmen, and noting for future reproof any instances of negligence, tyranny, or misconduct that took place within her observation. Men wondered how an ill-yoked chariot, a trodden and turbid watering-place, an over-loaded camel, all came under notice of the Great Queen; so that the prevalent belief in her godlike birth and more than human attributes gained ground day by day from these examples of a knowledge that seemed at once ubiquitous and infallible.

No sooner had she disposed her forces, with all the skill her experience suggested, round the stronghold of her enemy than she determined to examine for herself the actual state of the wall which fortified it, even if she had to venture within bow-shot of the defenders. For this purpose she stole from her own magnificent pavilion in the attire of an Assyrian archer, and covering her face as usual, passed slowly through the lines where the flower of an army lay encamped, which, though sadly weakened by the toil and hardships of its protracted march, seemed yet formidable antagonists to any power on earth.

The men were scattered about in groups, already making preparations, though noon was not long past, for their principal meal at sundown. Here a brawny warrior, with arms bared to the shoulder and legs to the thigh, was shredding herbs in his headpiece, the homeliness of his occupation contrasting ludicrously with the warlike nature of his cooking vessel, as did the nudity of his extremities with the proven harness that kept his mighty chest. A comrade, lying on his back with arms folded over his face, kicked his legs in the air, while he watched the proceedings with a listlessness that denoted he was for evening duty, and would have no share in the result. A score of others, ungirt, unsandalled, half-armed, half-dressed, were gathered round a dying camel, vociferating many opposing remedies for the poor beast's treatment, while the roar of an irritated stallion, the peal of a trumpet, the stamp and snort of a row of feeding horses, mingled with the hum of voices rising from a circle of stalwart warriors sitting, though the sun beat fiercely down, round the embers of their camp-fire.

It was not in the nature of Semiramis to pass these magnificent specimens of manhood without notice. Half unconsciously she lingered in their vicinity, marking their ample beards, fine stature, and robust proportions, agreeing well with their deep full tones, while they discussed freely enough the chances of the expedition and the stirring events of their daily life, sparing not the captains of ten thousand, nor forbearing to criticise the great leader herself, who stood by and overheard.

' 'Tis a strained bow they bid us bend, my brothers,' observed a scarred, war-worn veteran, whose mien and bearing displayed all the fierce pride, the overweening self-confidence assumed by those who had served under the Great King; 'a strained bow and a frayed cord—peradventure, a headless shaft to point, as well; but that makes little odds against solid masonry and bare rock. I doubt, if we are to get at the kernel of this date here over against us, we must crack the shell with our teeth.'

' I can tell thee that mine are blunt for want of use,' retorted a comrade, hammering busily at a broken link in his habergeon. ' How are men to be fed on the march through a country that grows nothing but oaks and brushwood? There is grass, indeed, between the hills, and game for those who can hunt it in the woods, but of corn and cattle the valleys are bare as the palm of my hand.'

'And empty as his belly,' laughed a third. 'He liketh well to have store of good things in both.'

'But Semiramis forbade pillage,' interposed his neighbour, grinning. 'They took an auxiliary with a shield full of barley that he snatched from an old man's threshing-floor, and she impaled him on the spot.'

'Fool! that was in our own land of Shinar, before we crossed the frontier,' said the first speaker. 'The Great Queen never forbade pillage in an enemy's country till we marched into this wilderness, where there is nothing to take. Besides, the rogue slew the old man in his own vineyard, and he was only an auxiliary after all.'

'And an ungainly wretch to boot, I will wager my share of supper presently out of that scanty pot,' added a handsome young spearman, arranging his curly beard in the breastplate he had polished up to the brightness of a mirror for that purpose. 'A comely youth of proper stature, be he captain or camel-driver, need never fear but he will find favour in the sight of the Great Queen.'

His fellows laughed loud and long.

'Hear him!' shouted one, clapping the speaker on the back, 'the favourite of Ashtaroth!'

'The dainty lotus-flower of the host!' exclaimed another; while a third, turning on him with mock gravity, bade him,

'Go to for a fool, who must be answered according to his folly.'

'Dost thou verily believe,' said he, 'that because of thy bull's head and shoulders, thy foolish leer like a sheep in a sacrifice, and the perpetual grin of a southern ape eating a sour pomegranate, thou wilt get preferment at her hands, who knows a man when she sees one, and treats him like the arrows in her quiver? Lo! the bow is bent, the mark is struck or missed, another is fitted to the string; but the same shaft never comes into her royal service again. Though thy turn of duty takes thee daily to the great pavilion, I doubt if the queen hath ever seen thee yet.'

'She shall hear of me, nevertheless,' said the other, with a glance at the beleaguered town.

'Knocking that empty head of thine against the wall!' returned the veteran. 'I tell ye, my brothers, that of all the wars yet undertaken by the sons of Ashur, this is the most untoward and ill-advised. What said the Great King when he turned back from the Zagros range, taking earth and water of the Men of the Mountain, but refraining to occupy their country? "I would be lord of all below," said he, pointing to those snow-whitened hills that mingle with the clouds, "while I leave to my fathers the dominion of the sky!" He has gone to join them at last; but could he come back to us this night, I tell ye by to-morrow's sunset we should be a day's march on our journey towards home!'

'Then why are we here now?' was asked by two or three voices at once.

The answer came in a grave important tone:

'Because of a treasure within those walls that Semiramis would wage life and empire, and you and me, and the whole might of Ashur to attain. What it is, I know not; if I knew, peradventure I dared not tell. But this I will uphold of the Great Queen, that her lightest wish is to the fixed resolve of another, as a man walking in armour to a maiden washing her feet in a stream.'

His listeners nodded approval, and scanning the lofty towers above them, began hazarding many conjectures as to the nature of that possession so coveted by their queen. A strong opinion seemed to prevail that Ardesh contained some illimitable store of spoils hoarded by Armenian kings for ages; and this impression served partly to counteract their general feeling of despondency and disheartening belief in the impregnable strength of the place. The youngest of these men of war spoke the most hopefully.

'I will never admit,' said he, 'that the might of man can shut out the sons of Ashur under the banner of our Great Queen. A rock is steep. Go to! shall we not cast a bank against it? A wall is thick; shall we not undermine it from beneath? Give me a high curved shield to keep my head, a steel pick, and an iron crowbar; behold, I will sit like a partridge in the barley, and burrow like a coney amongst the rocks.'

'So be it,' answered the veteran moodily. 'The sooner our trumpets sound to the assault the better. I tell thee, man, though the guards still show a goodly front, the hosts of Assyria are wasting and waning day by day, like that river in Egypt I passed over dry shod, like a flagon of Damascus wine, my brother, standing betwixt thee and me.'

The archer turned thoughtfully away, walking through the lines with folded hands and head bent down in earnest consideration.

There was food for reflection, even for anxiety and alarm, in the light talk of these careless spearmen.

When they touched on her personal weaknesses, her predilection for stalwart warriors, and especially her indomitable strength of will, the queen could not forbear a smile; but it faded into an expression of deeper gravity than was often worn by that bright face, while she pondered on the cost and peril of this adventurous expedition, so wild in its object, so disastrous in its results, confessing to her own heart that its impolicy was as obvious to her meanest followers as to their leader. Had not Assarac himself expressed the same opinion, almost in the same words?—Assarac, to whom she had never given a problem so hard but that he could solve it, a task so difficult, but that, for her sake, it was fulfilled.

Her armies melting away daily, her men of war dispirited and ill-supplied, a strongly-fortified city in front, a barren desert in rear! Not a captain of her host but would have quailed at the prospect, and had he been chief in command, would have commenced a fatal and disorderly retreat.

The character of Semiramis, however, was one on which danger and difficulty produced the effect of a hammer on glowing steel, welding and forging it, indeed, to the ends in view, but tempering it to an exceeding hardness and consistency the while. The desire of the present too, whatever it might be, became her master-passion for the time, and while sanguine and impetuous like a very woman, she possessed the courage, foresight, and obstinate perseverance of a man; also she enjoyed unlimited and irresponsible power as a queen; therefore it never entered her mind to abandon her task, or forego her intention of taking Sarchedon out of Ardesh by the strong hand, and marching the Comely King back to Babylon, a fettered captive at her chariot wheels.

'But to lie here inactive, waiting till he surrenders,' thought the queen, 'is like staring at ripe fruit in an orchard, till it drop down into the mouth. If a man hunger, let him climb the bough; I am but a woman, yet I think I can at least shake the tree.'

So she resolved that, at all hazards and all loss, the place must be carried by assault without delay. Thus musing, she passed through the vineyard occupied by her own archers to within an arrow's flight of the beleaguered fortress, unnoticed by those who believed her to be a simple bowman like themselves, and so proceeded to scan the wall, with an eye trained to detect the slightest point of advantage at a glance.

It was strong, very strong. Here, perhaps, a bank might be cast against it to some purpose; but the besiegers would suffer fearful slaughter in the work. There, covered by their large wicker shields, and plying their mining-tools, her heavy-armed spearmen might sap the foundations of the wall; but could they climb, and fight, and work, all at once, where there was scarce foothold for a goat? It must be done, nevertheless; but how to do it? She taxed her memory and her invention in vain.

Accident, however, came to her aid, when all her warlike skill was insufficient. Gazing steadfastly on the place, she marked the king's helmet drop from the wall, and her heart leaped with triumph when she beheld his bow-bearer, who recovered it, reascending with little difficulty to return it to his lord—with triumph, and with a sharper, keener, sweeter sensation still; for in that bow-bearer she recognised him for whom she was thus willing to risk life and empire; while the same glance revealed to her at once the desire of her eyes, and the path by which it was to be attained. She felt her cheek burn and her pulses throb; but even in that glowing moment, the instincts of the commander dominated those of the woman, and her brain was never clearer, nor her eye more accurate, than while she measured the height of the steep, and noted every fall of ground, every inequality of surface, that could be turned to account in moving the strength of her army at this point to the attack.

Ashtaroth, she knew, would always be ready to do her bidding, but it needed prudence, self-restraint, and a steadfast heart to force Merodach to her will.

CHAPTER VIII.

SONS OF THE SWORD.

On the brow of the Comely King lowered a cloud of anxiety and concern. He sat in the great stone hall of his rude palace, surrounded by chiefs and followers, to take counsel with them for the turning of this overwhelming tide, and foiling of the enemy at his gate.

Though, contrary to the custom of his nation, he rarely tasted wine himself, mighty flagons and capacious drinking-cups stood within each man's reach, so that while they pondered and stroked their beards, and shook their shaggy heads with ominous wisdom, many a deep draught was quaffed by these rugged heroes in silent pledge to the weapon they professed to worship, and of which they boasted themselves the offspring. In the middle of the hall, on a massiv stone altar, springing as it were from a groundwork of ferns and mosses, stood a naked broadsword, pointing to the roof; and not Baal himself, thought Sarchedon, in his stately temple at Babylon, with countless victims, streams of blood, libations of wine, and all the pomp of his white-robed priests, could have boasted a more sincere devotion than was offered by these rugged champions to the warlike symbol of their faith.

His bow-bearer stood on the king's right hand. It did not escape him that, although treated by Aryas with marked confidence and consideration, angry brows were bent and suspicious glances levelled at him from many in the assembly, who seemed to take exception at this promotion of an alien to such a post, more especially at a time when the stranger's own countrymen were pressing them so hard.

The haughty Assyrian winced and chafed under these symptoms of ill-will like a gallant steed, whose rider dare not trust his mettle, resolving that, ere long, some daring act of valour in the field should reinstate him in the good opinion of warriors, to whom success was a convincing proof of merit, and desperate courage the only test of worth.

To rush fiercely against the ranks of his own

nation, hewing, sword in hand, at the very men with whom he had heretofore broken bread in the city and marched to conquest in the field, went indeed sorely against the grain; but Sarchedon reflected that, besides the ties of gratitude which bound him to Aryas the Beautiful, there were many reasons, hardly less weighty, for his desertion from the banner of Ashur, and abandonment of his service under the Great Queen. To become once more a mere toy and plaything at the caprice of Semiramis was a thought too humiliating to be endured, even could he escape the usual doom of those on whom she cast a favouring-eye, while it was probable that she would at once take cruel vengeance for the vexation and disappointment of which he had been unwittingly the cause. So long as she remained mistress of the world, it was hopeless for him to think of honour and safety, above all, of Ishtar, liberty, and love. But if the Assyrian host could be defeated under the walls of Ardesh—if, baffled, scattered, and disorganised, they could be driven back on the rugged defiles and barren deserts that lay between them and their home—what was there to prevent an Armenian army from marching to the gates of Babylon? and how could Ishtar escape his search, who, at the conqueror's right hand, would scour the land of Shinar through its length and breadth, till he found the woman whom he had never ceased to love?

While such thoughts were teeming in his brain, he was not likely to endure with patience doubts of his fidelity to the cause he had espoused.

Many and opposite were the opinions of the warlike council. Saræus, a wealthy chieftain, arrayed with something more of luxury than his fellows, and lord of many a fertile valley beyond Mount Aragaz, as yet unoccupied and unheard of by the Assyrian, urged strenuously the prudence of standing a siege.

'We have fuel,' said he, 'we have shelter; casks of wine to broach, herds of beasts to slay. Let us eat, drink, and be merry, while the enemy perishes with hunger at our gates. The river runs between us, our walls are strong, our rocks are steep. Like the eagle on her eyrie, I would sit with folded wings and scream my defiance to the leopard prowling below.'

'Scream till thou art hoarse!' exclaimed Thorgon, a giant from the northern desert, armed in chain harness and clad in undressed skins, 'but remember, "He who hath the gullet of Saræus, should have his larder to keep it full."'

There was a general laugh at this application of a well-known proverb, founded on the wealth and fertility of the last speaker's dominions, and the luxurious habits of their owner. Thorgon proceeded, much pleased with the effect of his unaccustomed eloquence:

'When thy father summoned me to council, O king, he never paused to take my vote on a question of peace or war. Aramus knew and trusted his old comrade well. "Thorgon," said he, "is a steed always saddled, a bow always bent." I am ready, as I have ever been, to lead my long-swords into the fore-front of battle. But let not the king deceive himself: we have an enemy down yonder in the plain accustomed to conquer, inured to danger, skilled in all the arts and artifices of war. This is no broad-leafed oak into which we must drive the old Armenian wedge, but a front of solid earth-fast rock!'

Men looked in each other's faces, discouraged and alarmed. It was something new to hear this fiery patriarch express doubts of victory. A hint of caution from Thorgon was tantamount to forebodings of defeat from milder spirits; and a short but ominous silence fell on the assembled council, while each realised the danger he had hitherto shrunk from acknowledging even to himself.

It was broken by the king.

'There is a courage to endure,' said he, 'as there is a courage to assail. When the snow-winds come, they will rid us of our enemy, without bending of bow or shaking of spear. But our grapes are yet green in the vineyards, our barley scarce whitening on the plain. How many days, think you, my brothers, will meat and drink be forthcoming if we elect to remain up here, cooped within the walls of Ardesh like a swarm of bees in a hive?'

Again opinions varied; some thought they might hold out a hundred, some barely a score. Thorgon offered to break through the lines of the enemy, and bring in sheep and horses from the wind-swept plains of his home.

'When we have eaten the last down to their hoofs,' growled the fierce warrior, 'we can always run out, sword in hand, and take what we want from the tether ropes of this scolding housewife whom they call the Great Queen!'

'Sarchedon,' said Aryas, turning to his bow-bearer, 'you have held your peace too long. Give us your counsel, man; for you best know the strength and the designs of our enemy.'

There was a stir in the hall at this appeal to the stranger, and more than one sword leaped a hand's-breadth from its scabbard. Murmurs of 'Traitor, traitor!' rose by degrees to louder outcries. 'Out with him!' 'Down with him!' 'Slay him and cast him over the wall to his own people, who have come hither at his desire!' were the mildest of these revilings, while a scuffling of feet and crowding of shoulders about his place at the king's right hand denoted no good-will to the Assyrian, small chance of mercy or even justice if national prejudice and panic should get the upper hand. Aryas flushed dark red with anger; but Thorgon interposed his massive person between the bow-bearer and those who threatened him, while his deep hoarse voice cried 'Shame!' in accents that might have been heard by the besiegers outside.

'A stranger, and treated thus in the king's council-chamber!' he shouted. 'By the sword that begot our nation, I will stamp the life out of the first man who steps across the hall! What! the Assyrian came to our gates a captive and a suppliant, and shall we deliver him up, were he ten times a traitor, at the bidding of the loudest-tongued shrew that ever wore a smock? Nay, my brothers, stand back, I say; give every man a fair hearing, and room to swing a sword!'

Thus adjured, the assembly subsided into their places, and Sarchedon took advantage of restored order to protest earnestly against the suspicions of those with whom he had come to dwell.

'I am an Assyrian,' said he, facing boldly round on such as had been most vehement in their outcries, 'and I am proud of my birth as of my nation. But I was also a soldier of the Great King, who could never be urged to war within the confines of Armenia, and I owe no allegiance to her who has taken unlawful possession of his throne, who would establish herself thereon with tyranny and injustice. I came here a weary footsore slave; I was fed, comforted, and raised to honour by my lord the king. Every drop of my blood shall be poured out to do him service. Bethink ye too, Men of the Mountain, if the Assyrian takes me fighting in your ranks, he will strip the skin from my body to make sandals for his feet. Those strike fierce and hard who have no retreat; and if honour, good faith, gratitude, count for nothing, at least you may trust him for whom defeat is a cruel and shameful death. My lord the king hath demanded my counsel. To so noble an assembly it is not for me to offer advice, but I am enabled to give information. I have returned but a short space from the outer wall. Since daybreak the enemy hath been busied in turning the course of the river, that he may advance to the assault dry shod. You yourselves best know to what purpose you can defend the city from an attack on its weaker side; but my lord the king hath demanded counsel of his servant, and it is not for me to shrink from speaking because of angry threats and scowling brows. Were I King Aryas of Armenia, as I am his faithful bow-bearer, I would go down to battle with the Assyrian, and strive with him, man to man, outside the city-walls!'

Loud shouts of applause greeted this daring speech, and Thorgon, striding across the hall, laid his broad hand on the Assyrian's shoulder, with a gesture of unqualified approval and respect. The enthusiasm became general, so that even Saræus shouted and gesticulated with the rest; but Aryas, stepping proudly into the midst, drew his sword from its sheath, and kissing its handle, raised its point towards the roof. Each man present followed his example, and thus, with naked weapons gleaming in their hands, they listened in silence to the words of the Comely King.

'It is well spoken!' said he. 'Surely the bow-bearer hath shot his arrow home to the mark. If indeed the river be turned, steep rock and solid wall will avail us little against the huge engines and innumerable archers of the Assyrian. It is wise to attack when it seems hopeless to defend; and who shall stand against Armenia coming down in her might, like one of her own torrents from the snow-topped hills? I am a free king, ruling over a free people, yet can I count on you, my friends and followers, as on the steel in my own right hand. Let us set the battle in array, and fight the quarrel to the death. The stranger never turned from our father's gate in peace, nor entered it in war. Shall we forget whose sons we are to-day, because of a fierce people, riding on horses, worshipping strange gods, and mustering countless as the snowflakes in a storm? I call on you, as Aramus would have called on your fathers, to rally round his son; and I pledge you in that sacred cup to which, since Armenia became a nation, traitor or coward hath never dared to lay his lips!'

With these words, the king filled a mighty bowl with wine, and bringing the edge of his sword so briskly across his naked fore-arm that the blood spouted from the gash, suffered a few drops to drain into the liquid; then, raising the vessel to his lips, drank heartily ere he passed the bowl to Thorgon, who, following his example, sent it round amongst the rest, each man quaffing his share with the zeal and gravity of one who partakes in a religious rite. When at last the bowl reached Sarchedon, there was scarce a mouthful left; but the Assyrian, catching the spirit of this strange ceremony, pierced his own arm without hesitation, and thus pledged his new comrades in a draught of blood.

Any lingering suspicions they might have entertained were completely dissipated by so ready a compliance with their ancient custom, and not one but went out from the presence of his lord to prepare for battle with a confidence as implicit in the fidelity of the stranger as in his own.

With measured steps, lowered weapons, and a grave aspect, as having before them a task it would tax all their strength to accomplish, these Men of the Mountain departed one by one, each, as he left the hall, turning with grim salute to do obeisance to the Naked Sword. When the last had vanished, Sarchedon, looking into the face of his lord, felt his heart sink and his blood run cold; for on the brow of the Comely King, though courageous and serene as ever, there was imprinted the seal of the destroyer—there seemed to sit that cloud, so awful and so mysterious, which is the shadow of coming death.

CHAPTER IX.

FAITHFUL UNTO DEATH.

'IT is our only course against such a foe,' said Aryas, after a gloomy silence, during which lord and servant seemed to have been following out no cheering train of thought. 'For any nation on earth to oppose thy countrymen in warfare is to wield a shepherd's staff against a blade of tempered steel. But one heavy blow from the club, well-aimed and unexpected, may sometimes shiver the deadlier weapon to its hilt. Our long swords of the mountain bite sharp and true. The wedge of Armenia can pierce a column, however dense, and the gap widens as we fight on. Surely it will cleave the might of Assyria, as a woodman's axe cleaves the sturdy oak of the hills.'

'But the oak is rooted to its place,' objected Sarchedon, 'while the Assyrian can wheel and stoop and strike like a falcon in the air. His horsemen will open out, and bend their bows till they have wrapped the advancing wedge in a storm of deadly hail—till its men fall thick, and its might is loosened from the rear. Then will Semiramis order up her war-chariots on either flank; and, once broken, as well he knows, there is no rallying for the long swords of my lord the king.'

'They shall *not* be broken,' exclaimed Aryas. 'With Thorgon to lead them on foot, with their king to direct the battle in his chariot, with thy skill of warfare, Sarchedon, and our own good cause, I commit the result to that power which hath ever befriended Armenia, in attack and in defence — the might of the Naked Sword. Yet I would we could fight them at a vantage, nevertheless,' he added, his enthusiasm changing to deep anxiety and concern. 'Their armour, their weapons, their horses, are better than ours, and they outnumber us ten to one.'

'True, O king!' replied Sarchedon; 'therefore must we fall upon them unawares. Behold! In their ranks every spearman hath been taught to handle spade, every slinger uses the pick deftly as he whirls the thong, each third man carries a mattock or a shovel; and the Great Queen values their labour no dearer than their lives. This night one half her host will be employed to turn the course of the river that keeps your city on its eastern side. Let my lord the king summon his men of war in the hours of darkness, and at daybreak go down to battle. If he conquer, it will be with the first onslaught. If he fail, then may Sarchedon, his friend and servant, pay back the life he owes, and die at his lord's feet.'

Again that ominous shadow passed over the king's face: he laid his hand kindly on the other's shoulder, and spoke in a low sad voice.

'Sarchedon,' said he, 'when I shielded thee from the demand of an Assyrian embassy, it was for jealousy of my father's honour—for the cause of the stranger and the oppressed. When I took thee out from under thy horse—ay, from off the very horns of the wild bull—it was for care of a faithful servant risking life at the pleasure of his lord. Now we are master and slave, crowned king and belted bow-bearer no more, but friends in esteem and affection, brothers in confidence and love. I tell thee that the days of Aryas, the son of Aramus, are numbered, and the mountain men must choose them another king to guide their counsels and lead their long swords into battle. Last night I dreamed a dream; and it needs no wise man, no cunning soothsayer, to read the interpretation thereof. Behold, I was hunting in the mountain, riding to and fro with bow in hand and hound in leash, seeking to take a prey. In vain I traversed hill and valley, rock and river, stately forest and scattered copse—leaf, grass, and flower were alike scathed and blighted. It seemed that a flight of locusts had passed over all. Then I cursed the nakedness of the land in my wrath; and while thrice I shouted "Barren, barren, barren!" mine own voice sounded hideous in mine ears. So I rode slowly on, and beneath my horse's feet I beheld three things that caused my blood to curdle and the hair of my flesh to stand on end.

'The first was a slain eagle pierced by a headless shaft; the second was a wild bull noosed in a woman's girdle; the third was a dead man lying on his face with the king's sandals on his feet, the king's baldrick on his shoulders, and the king's quiver at his back. I tell thee, Sarchedon, the warning lies betwixt thee and me. Let us drink a cup of wine in fellowship to-night; for if we go down to battle with to-morrow's dawn, one of us shall have quenched his thirst for ever by noon of day.'

'On my head may it fall!' exclaimed Sarchedon.

'Let the slave perish, and let his lord, who raised him from the dust, ride forth to victory!'

'Nay, hear me,' replied the king; 'for I have already told thee lord and slave are no words between Aryas and Sarchedon. If I accept the vision for myself, I am willing to face its interpretation freely as I would face the horsemen of Assyria and the chariots of the Great Queen. I might die many a baser death than to fall in battle with Thorgon and his long swords at my back. But if it is for thee that the dream has been sent, I tell thee, my faithful friend and comrade, I cannot bear to think that thy share in our joint venture should be all loss and no gain. When I took thee into my palace, rude and homely though it seem, I swore its halls should be a harness of proof and a tower of defence for the stranger who sought its shelter. When I gave thee a place in my heart, I resolved I would bring thee to promotion and honour—not to danger, defeat, and death. Go out from among us, Sarchedon, ere it be too late. Return, as of thine own free will, to the Assyrian, with fair words and costly gifts. Buy their favour and the safety of thy body with that fair province of the south that lies by the Glassy Lake. Behold, it is a gift from me to thee. Tell them that the open hand of

Aryas is heavy as his clenched fist. Bid the Great Queen depart in peace; but if she must needs come to buffets, there is space enough to fight a kingly battle beneath the walls of Ardesh. If she desires to seize my father's crown, she must take it off my brows by force where I stand, in my war-chariot armed with bow and spear.'

For all answer, Sarchedon stripped the quiver from his shoulders, took the sword from his thigh, and laid the weapons at his lord's feet.

'It is enough,' said he. 'If the king can believe his servant capable of thus ransoming one poor life at the cost of honour, I have served him already too long. There are many brave men among his subjects better fitted than Sarchedon for the highest post Armenia has to offer. Poor and naked as he came, let the Assyrian return to the station from which he was raised by the favour of my lord the king. Yet, if true service and a grateful heart may plead for him, even now he will but ask to take his place to-morrow in the fore-front of battle, and, habited like a simple soldier of Aryas, march with the Men of the Mountain to his death.'

The king's features worked with emotion. 'Not so,' he exclaimed in hoarse and broken accents.

'True and faithful servants I can number by scores, but such a heart as this cleaveth to a man, be he king or herdsman, once in a lifetime. Surely it sticketh faster than a brother. I have proved thee, Sarchedon, as one proves the harness that is to keep his life. I tell thee, we will go down to battle side by side; together we will bend the bow and point the javelin. Honour, danger, and triumph we will share alike; and when the end comes, as something warns me come it will, peradventure in death we shall not be divided.'

Then he lifted belt and baldrick from the stones, and with his own hand fastened the quiver at Sarchedon's back, girt the sword on his thigh, thus reinstating the bow-bearer in all the honours he had voluntarily resigned.

Standing side by side in this reversal of their relative positions, it chanced that the servant caught sight of his own figure and his master's reflected in the burnished surface of an empty wine-flagon over against them. Remarking, not for the first time, their extraordinary similarity of form and features, Sarchedon now ventured on a request that only the high favour in which he stood, and the humility of his tone while proffering it, could have rendered palatable to his listener.

'Let not the king be wroth with his servant,' said he, hesitating, like one who tries a plank with his foot ere he commits to it the whole of his weight, 'if he ask yet another proof, in addition to all the honours heaped on him, of the trust in which he is held by his lord. Behold, like the sand that sucks the desert spring, he thirsteth yet for more! Let the king grant him the desire of his heart, and live for ever!'

'Say on, man!' replied Aryas, somewhat impatiently; 'surely there needs not all this ceremony between thee and me. By to-morrow's sunset,' he added, in a lower, sadder tone, 'the same wild dog may be scaring the vultures from us both.'

'Then, if we are to meet our death together,' replied Sarchedon, 'let it be in the same habit and the same armour. This is the boon I earnestly beg of my lord to grant. Men have said, ere now, that armed and in the field there is some such resemblance between Sarchedon and him who is called Aryas the Beautiful, as between the illusive verdure of the desert and those groves and waters that it represents. Let me take upon me then to array myself in such attire and harness as are worn by my lord the king; so, in the press of battle, the advantage of his presence and conduct shall be double, while the risk from his enemies—for my people strike ever at the head—will be but half.'

Aryas pondered.

'And if I fall,' said he, 'wilt thou bring on the Men of the Mountain like a free Armenian king, leading the long swords to the charge again and again, even unto death?'

'I will do my best,' replied the other; 'for, indeed, whither am I to retreat? and what will be my fate if I am made a captive? Surely I have nothing to fear but defeat. If the long swords will follow, I ask no better than to lead them through the ranks of Assyria—to the very chariot of the Great Queen!'

The king's eyes blazed with unwonted fire.

'Swear it!' he exclaimed vehemently.

'I swear it by the everlasting wings!' answered Sarchedon; and so they made their compact with death.

CHAPTER X.

A FOOL IN HIS FOLLY.

It is not to be supposed that the warlike skill which assisted Ninus to form his plans, and the courage which rivalled his own in carrying them out, would fail Semiramis now that she was unfettered by the counsels and commands of her lord. The sons of Ashur had never yet been led so judiciously, organised so carefully, as in this daring expedition to the north, under conduct of the Great Queen.

Aryas little knew with whom he had to deal, when he spoke of surprising her by sudden onslaught, or hoped to rout her in the fury of his attack. Her watchmen were posted, her defences prepared, her dispositions made to meet his wiliest stratagems; and all the time, while every working-party was covered by a guard of twice its number, the labour progressed steadily, and the river, on which the besieged chiefly depended for security, waned, cubit by cubit and hour by hour.

None knew better than this woman-warrior how the presence of a commander infuses spirit into the operations of an army, how the ubiquity of a leader promotes that attention to details which alone insures success: there was no period of the day or night but the queen's white horse might be seen flitting through the lines of her innumerable host, while the lovely face smiled its calm approval, or expressed displeasure, no less fatal because so grave and quiet; always pale, immovable, and serene, under gleam of moonlight, flash of torches, or glare of day.

Men wondered when she ate and slept, inclining to believe that this supernatural beauty must be above such human wants, tended and nourished by the stars from whence it came.

Only Assarac perhaps, in all that host, knew too well that the Great Queen's passions and affections were of earth, earthly; that the flame which scorched her heart and blazed in her eyes was no enlightening radiance, but a devouring fire to wither and consume—knew too well, yet loved her all the more; for the eunuch's whole being was now saturated with a sentiment noble in its origin, disastrous in its results, that yet springs from the fairest and sweetest instincts of man's nature, as poison may be distilled from flowers.

It caused him to labour and watch, to endure hunger, thirst, heat, and fatigue. It bade him forget pride, ambition, self-respect. It made him a warrior, a hero, and a slave. It rendered him brave, pitiful, generous, and unhappy.

Twice since sundown had the queen ridden out through the camp, with Assarac at her rein. Once more she was astir an hour before daybreak, yet, as she mounted at the entrance of her pavilion, the eunuch stood there in waiting to help her to the saddle, and attend her in her ride. Without a word she galloped through the lines, at such speed as the dubious light permitted amongst the numerous obstacles of a camp, nor drew bridle till she reached a spot by the river, where certain masses of shadows looming against the sky denoted that the walls of Ardesh would be visible with dawn of day. Here she halted and broke silence.

'A city of defence,' said she with a gentle laugh, 'like a blade, or a pitcher, or a woman, or anything else you please, is no stronger than its weakest place.

On this side alone is Ardesh not impregnable. I have made thee a warrior, Assarac, as a girl spins her hank out of a tangle of flax, with the patient heart and the gentle hand. Show me thou hast profited by my lessons, and tell me why I brought thee here at a gallop before dawn.'

Brightening as he always did with the sound of her voice, Assarac answered, reasonably enough, 'To scan the place warily as soon as it is light; to learn every bush and stone, count every blade of grass on the ground where we mean to give the assault.'

'Not so,' she answered, in the same light tone. 'All that was done in this poor head of mine when first I marked the spot. No; the warrior-eunuch has yet much to learn from the warrior-queen. It is not enough to set your own host in array, and mark your own plan of battle; you must also fight for your enemy, put yourself in his place, and so, anticipating him in every plan he can devise, force him at last to accept the contest when and where you choose to offer it. The reason women always foil men is, that they *cannot* put themselves in our places, nor foresee what we may or may not do in the plainest situation. But this concerns neither thee nor me. I think I have even less of the woman than thou, Assarac, of the man.'

He answered not a word, moving uneasily in his saddle, as if from a sudden hurt.

'Nay,' she added, guessing his discomposure from his silence; 'I meant we are both above the weaknesses of our fellows—kindred spirits treading down all obstacles in our path, knowing no law but our own will and our own desires. Listen, then, thou priest of Baal in harness of proof—listen, and learn while I teach thee that which shall be of more service to-day than all the lore aching neck and dazzled eyes ever yet gathered from the stars. Is not this the weak side of the fortress, and therefore the better for our assault?'

'Aryas must know it also,' replied the eunuch, 'and will have mustered here his chief power of defence. Peradventure we might surprise him, with less loss, on a stronger quarter.'

'An apt scholar,' replied the queen, 'and worthy to be a captain of ten thousand; nevertheless, in so far at fault that he sees not with the eyes of his enemy. Behold! The Armenian, hopeless of defending his city from such a host as mine in the process of a regular siege, and seeing the river in which he trusted turning to dry ground beneath his eyes, will determine to hazard a battle here on this narrow strip where he can fight at a vantage, while half the attacking army is engaged with pickaxe and spade. Listen, priest. I hear the tinkle of their tools even now, borne on the light breeze that steals in advance of day. He little guesses the work was all completed by the middle watch of night; that every company is bending, armed, over a feigned task in order of battle; that, at the first note of a trumpet from the queen's pavilion, be it dark or daylight or gray uncertain dawn, the hosts of Assyria will set themselves in array without hesitation or confusion, every bow bent, every horse mounted, every man in his place.

'Since my tent was pitched yonder by the stream, I have not found a moment till now to breathe the cool night air and loose the buckle of my belt. Is it not grand and joyous, this pause before the storm? At such a moment I feel how noble it is to lead the sons of Ashur to battle. To-night, Assarac, I *know* that I am the Great Queen!'

She seldom thus divulged her own thoughts, her own sentiments. The tones of that voice, always so bewitching, thrilled to his heart's core; and with irrepressible admiration he burst out, 'Queen of the sons of Ashur! Queen of the whole earth! Were there indeed crowns of fire above, queen of the host of heaven! What have I to offer in earnest of such devotion as never worshipper yielded to his god? It is little enough to give this poor brain in council, this poor body in battle; but O that I could take the heart out of my breast now, this moment, and lay it down before thee there, to trample beneath thy feet!'

'It is too much,' she answered, almost in a whisper. 'I may tread warriors in the dust, but I make no footstool of a servant's heart, be he man of war, eunuch, or priest of Baal. Keep it in thy harness, good friend, and see that to-day it turn not to water in the face of the Comely King.'

Dawn was still below the mountain, and he could not read her countenance; but on his ear, sharpened by intense emotion, there jarred a something in her voice that broke its full melodious ring. Was it kindness? Was it pity? Maddening thought! was it the insult of covert mirth?

'I am not like others,' said he. 'I know it too well; and yet my adoration of my queen is less the blind man's yearning for the day he hath never seen than that desire of the spirit for some star it must not hope to attain, which yet raises it, by the very agony of its despair, towards the light for which it longs.'

She had a brief space of leisure before the joyous revelry of battle would commence. There was no better pastime, she thought, at hand. Why not examine into so strange a phase of human suffering, and learn how much the heart, even of such a man as this, could be made to bear, before it maddened him past all endurance? Surely such studies, so curious in themselves, enhanced the flavour of that pursuit she dignified with the name of love; a pursuit far inferior, no doubt, to war, equal though, and perhaps in very hot weather preferable, to the chase. Here a memory of Sarchedon came to disturb her equanimity; but so much of bitterness and vexation mingled with the thought, that her heart grew all the harder for its indulgence. What had she to do with pity, she who had slain beasts by scores and men by hundreds to pass an idle day? Had she ever wished her shaft recalled when it pierced the lion through from shoulder to shoulder; and were these human creatures half so brave, so noble as the brutes? Was she not the Great Queen, answerable to none on earth, and fearless of the very stars in heaven? Besides, it amused—more, it interested—her. So she, the conqueror of the world, thought no shame to trifle with him as a village maid trifles with her peasant lover, as a cat trifles with its paltry little prey.

'There is a light,' she said, reverting gently to his wild confession of idolatry, 'that blinds a man's eyes, besides burning his fingers. It is not that by which he sees his way clearly to safety or success.'

'And of what avail are safety and success to *me?*' demanded Assarac, striving in the early twilight to read his doom on that remorseless face. 'Success, the prize of him who hopes; safety, the desire of him who fears. If I am below hope, surely I am also above fear. My queen, look on that shadowy mass of wall and tower, darkening every moment against the coming light of dawn. How many bold warriors, think you, are within that city who to-day will draw the sword and throw away the scabbard once for all? I too have drawn the sword and rushed upon my fate. Like one who leaps into air from the tower of Belus, I cannot recall my plunge. Great Queen, I have dared to love the very dust beneath your feet. Here, in the day of battle, I dare to tell you so. Ere set of sun, Semiramis shall be ruler over all the world, from the warm river of Egypt to the bleak snow-deserts of the north; or Assarac shall be down in the strife of horsemen, trodden out of all likeness to humanity. Enough! I can but serve her at the end as I have served her from the beginning; and for wages I do but ask, great glorious queen, look kindly on me ere I die!'

His voice came hoarse and broken, his smooth face worked convulsively from chin to eyebrows. Surely any other woman must have been moved—at least to compassion; but Semiramis, pulling her horse's head up from the wet morning herbage he was cropping with avidity, gazed intently on the walls of Ardesh, now visible in the light of dawn.

Was not the great stake for which she played enclosed within those towers, the desire of her eyes, the treasure of her wilful heart? She could understand, she thought, those longings on which the eunuch laid such stress, but of pity, save for her own sufferings, she had none to spare.

'Listen!' exclaimed the queen, turning round on her companion with one hand held in air, as though she had not heard a syllable of his appeal, 'they are mustering even now within the place. Stand still,

Merodach! Good horse, the ring of steel stirs thee like thy mistress! What say you, Assarac—can we creep on a bow-shot nearer to make sure? The light is behind them, and we may defy their archers for a few moments yet.'

Thus speaking, she moved her horse forward a score of paces, followed by the priest, vexed, smarting, dizzy with anger and shame.

But his tortures were not over, his punishment not yet complete. Sitting calmly on her horse, though day was breaking fast, and every instant brought nearer the certainty of a storm of arrows from the wall, Semiramis looked round with a careless smile, like some light-minded dame chattering with her tirewoman.

'What think you, Assarac?' she whispered. 'Is he waking yet, this Comely King?—of whose beauty they make such a prate you would suppose he was Shamash, god of day. I would fain see him rise from his couch; for I like well to look on beauty, both of man and beast.'

Then she patted Merodach on his swelling neck, sighing and smiling too while she caressed her favourite: the sigh was for memory, the smile for triumph and for hope.

'We shall rouse him to some purpose,' answered the eunuch, mastering his emotion bravely. 'And the Great Queen shall judge of his beauty for herself, naked and a prisoner, bound at her chariot-wheels.'

He spoke firmly, even gaily, as behoved one who had made up his mind for the worst. That day, he resolved, should see the end of all this doubt, and longing, and misery. In the front of battle he would perform such deeds of valour as should force the queen's regard for *him*, the eunuch, who could thus put to shame her stoutest men of war, or in the ranks of the long swords he would find out the great secret, and start for yonder place, wherever it might be, that Ninus and Sargon, and so many others, had reached long ago.

Semiramis caught up her rein with an exclamation of delight.

'I was sure of it!' she said; 'I knew it from the first! They will fight in the plain—they are moving the host down even now. Behold, I can see their archers on the wall! It is time for you and me, Assarac, to prove the mettle of our horses and the surety of their archers' aim.'.

As she spoke, she urged Merodach to a gallop, while an arrow whistling by her cheek quivered in the ground a spear's length farther on. The good horse only sped the faster, and ere morning had brightened the mountain's crest, Semiramis reached her pavilion, and her trumpets rang gaily out, to set the sons of Ashur in array.

CHAPTER XI.

BOW AND SPEAR.

It was a goodly sight, could the queen have waited to behold it, that downward march of the Armenian host to meet their enemy in the plain. The flower and pride of all the north, formidable in size, number, and length of weapons, they deployed, squadron by squadron, and company by company, under cover of their archers on the wall, till they found space near the river's empty bed to form that wedge, or solid triangle, in which it was their custom to offer battle. This mass consisted of spearmen, who with levelled points and raised bucklers seemed to present but an impervious hedge of steel to the efforts of an adversary. It was designed to penetrate and cleave asunder by sheer weight and pressure the opposing force, while Thorgon and his long swords, mounted on their swift hardy horses, held themselves in readiness to cut up and destroy in detail the fragments of an enemy thus riven the wider the more it gave ground to its assailants.

Such a method of fighting was considered by the mountain men to insure victory; and the queen's eye sparkled, her cheek glowed, when she beheld the hosts of Aryas the Beautiful thus eager to engage her own on a system of which she had mastered all the details, prepared to worst it at every point.

'The lion is astir,' she said, 'and walking deliberately into the toils without an effort at escape. By the light of Astaroth, I will have his claws pared, his fangs drawn, and the beast as tame as a kitten, before close of day!'

Splendidly armed, ablaze with gold and jewels that flashed in the morning sun, she stood in her chariot, looking like the goddess by whom she swore, her beautiful face radiant with pleasure, her heart beating high with courage, triumph, and the wild tumult of unbridled love.

Her shield-bearer's place still remained vacant, and save a youth to drive her horses, she was alone in the chariot; for Assarac, who remained as usual in attendance, occupied another at her side.

The eunuch's face was very grave and sad; its

fleshy outlines had fallen, the eyes were sunk and haggard, while about the lips care and sorrow had carved those anxious lines that age itself fails to imprint when the heart remains at ease.

He looked little like a priest of Baal, less like a warrior of Ashur; but never prophet burned with fiercer fire, never were nerves of champion strung to more desperate courage, than glowed in the vexed heart and wounded spirit of Assarac the eunuch, thus waiting on Semiramis the queen.

He had galloped back with her to the camp before sunrise, and at the first trumpet-call ascended into his chariot, that he might aid her with his counsel, perhaps shield her with his body in the press of battle.

In the disposal of her power she had shown her accustomed skill. Dark masses of horsemen gathered like clouds on either flank. Her spearmen, in a solid column, occupied the centre, protecting a bristling array of war-chariots, ready to be launched against the enemy so soon as he advanced into the plain; while forming her own guard and a reserve to be hurled, as it were, at the critical moment on any point she should select, rode a picked body of warriors clothed in blue, shining with gilded armour and chosen from the flower of her men of war by the queen herself.

Aryas the Beautiful, surveying from his chariot the line of battle thus opposed to him, felt, while his courage rose with its very hopelessness, a sad conviction of the impossibility of his task. He whispered as much to Sarchedon, who accompanied him.

'Behold,' said he, 'how the wolves are gathering to hem in the mountain bull on every side. I knew not they were so many, nor so fierce. Surely he is a daring leader who joins battle with the sons of Ashur.'

The other, while acknowledging so obvious a truth, could not repress a thrill of exultation in the fair and formidable array of warriors with whom he had heretofore gone out to victory.

At the same moment Semiramis turned to Assarac, whose chariot now stood by her own, and pointed with a radiant smile to those long lines of steel glittering in the morning sun.

'The blade is out,' said she, 'and balances so well in my hand, I can smite when and where I will. Who would care to be a queen, but that the arm which sways a sceptre has such strength to draw a sword? Behold, the very auxiliaries stand fast, as if they too felt they carried on their spears the honour of Assyria!'

'Trust not their patience too far,' urged the eunuch. 'Great Queen, they are clamouring to engage even now!'

'Fools,' she returned gaily, 'I mean to sacrifice them soon enough. But I can scarce trust them in the first shock of the assault, or I would leave our own people to come in and reap the victory.'

'Let not the Great Queen scorn the words of her servant,' replied Assarac, 'humble man of peace though he be. The children of Anak, led by their woman-captain, claim the advance as their right. Behold, they are fierce champions, tall as palms, greedy as beasts of prey, acknowledging no law save the customs of their tribe. How shall these be satisfied when the fight is over, the victory gained, and the spoil divided? Grant them their wish: let them hurl themselves against the enemy. If they loosen his formation, it is well; if they turn back in confusion while he smites them hip and thigh, it is better. Assyria can do without them in the day of triumph as in the day of battle.'

The queen scanned him from head to foot.

'Do you think I cannot rein a steed,' she asked,

with a scornful laugh, 'because it is strong and wilful, or rule a handful of horsemen because they stand a span higher than their fellows? Go to, Assarac; I thought you knew me better. I have a task in store for these same Anakim, and I purpose leading them myself. They shall help me to take this Comely King captive from the very midst of his host. I tell you, I mean to look at his beautiful face before sunset, as close as I am to you!'

'May the queen live for ever!' was his reply, for Assarac's whole attention seemed now engrossed by the strength of Armenia advancing to the attack.

The wedge came on, solid and impenetrable as if it were indeed a living mass of metal. Thus it crossed the level ground by the river's bed, directing its point steadily for the centre of the Assyrian line; and so long as it moved upon an even surface, nothing could be more warlike than the mechanical regularity of its advance—nothing, perhaps, save the discipline of the Assyrian archers, whom the queen kept so perfectly in hand, that in spite of a tempting proximity to the Armenians, not a man moved in his saddle, turned his rein, or bent his bow. But when the huge triangular phalanx reached the channel, now dried up indeed, yet rough with broken banks, sandy ledges, shingle, and boulders of rock, a shiver seemed to pass over it like that which ripples the hide of some huge monster in its death-pang, and Aryas drove furiously down in his chariot to rectify the disorder ere it was too late.

In compliance with his bow-bearer's entreaties, the attire and harness of the Comely King, though less simple than usual, were such as might be worn by any captain or leader of his host. There was nothing about him to identify his royalty but the handsome form and face. Sarchedon also was armed and dressed in a precisely similar manner, so that at the interval of a spear-length it was impossible to distinguish one from the other. The bow-bearer too had divested himself of the quiver that denoted his office, and while he stood upright, and brandished a spear in the war-chariot, Aryas covered him with a shield. Even old Thorgon, riding up to his lord for final orders, rubbed his eyes and pulled his shaggy beard in angry confusion at its success, while he admitted the wisdom of this stratagem.

With voice and gesture, Aryas and Sarchedon strove in concert to restore that dense consistency to the mass which constituted its strength and safety; but eyes as quick, and skill more practised, were watching their opportunity, so that as the leading Armenian spearman made his first false step, the arm of Semiramis went up, a trumpet sounded, and the horsemen of Assyria set themselves in motion by thousands, with bows bent and arrows drawn to the head.

There is a moment, and none knew it better than the Great Queen, on which the tide of battle turns.

'In the toils *now!*' she murmured viciously, 'and that fair head of yours will be at my mercy to-night, as sure as I hold this bow in my hand. Assarac,' she continued, in the calm ringing accents with which it was her wont to issue her commands in battle, 'let them feed that force of archers thousands by thousands, as they want them, from the columns on their flanks. When the Armenian host arrives at yonder white stone, bring up the reserve of spearmen, and I will attack with the whole line.'

Ere this landmark could be reached, she was well aware that the advancing phalanx, stumbling at every step, galled on all sides by mounted bowmen, who, circling swiftly round, wrapped it in a deadly storm of arrows, must become so loosened and disorganised as with one well-supported charge to be broken up and cut to pieces in detail.

Already darting an upward glance at the towers of Ardesh, she was doubting whether to occupy it with a strong Assyrian garrison or to burn its palace, and level its defences to the ground. For a space all went as she desired. Wheeling in clouds, succeeded and relieved by squadron after squadron, each fresher, fiercer, more daring than the last, it seemed to Aryas that the horsemen of Assyria were inexhaustible and intangible as the locusts of their own fertile land. With each discharge of arrows, his phalanx hesitated, tottered, and opened out. It was no longer a solid wedge, but an irregular mass, melting and crumbling like a snow-wreath in the southern breeze. There was not a moment to lose, and the Comely King, whose habits of wood-craft had at least gifted him with that promptitude of decision which is so necessary in war, saw the crisis and prepared to meet it.

'Sarchedon,' he exclaimed, 'leap on my horse, the bay standing there behind the chariot! Ride down to Thorgon like the wind. Bid him bring up his long swords steadily, but without delay. At the first step taken by the enemy's spearmen, he must charge and drive them back amongst their chariots. It is the last chance left. Away! Two Armenian kings are fighting side by side this morning; Sarchedon, if at set of sun there is but one left, my faithful friend and servant, fare thee well!'

Touching his lord's hand reverently with his lips, the bow-bearer flung himself into the saddle, and galloped off at speed; while Aryas, snatching reins and whip from his charioteer, shaking the former and plying the latter to some purpose, flew towards that white stone which the keen eye of Semiramis had already marked as the turning-point of conflict.

When they parted, scarce a bow-shot intervened between the king's chariot and the handful of Anakim who were drawn up in the position they had clamoured to occupy, waiting with fiery impatience an order to begin.

Their queen sat motionless at their head, her face concealed as usual, her eyes intently scanning those hostile ranks in search of the man she loved.

Suddenly she dropped the rein and clasped her hands upon her heart. Surely that was his figure yonder, riding, as he alone could ride, along the river bank! A dead archer lay in his path, and the bay horse, swerving wildly aside, brought his rider round with a swing that showed his front to the enemy.

'Sarchedon, Sarchedon!' she cried in a stifled voice, then stretched her arms out piteously, and, gasping for breath, flung the veil back from her face.

It was the signal they had expected since daybreak, the gesture by which they were taught to believe their enemies would be consumed like thorns crackling in a fire. The wild blood of the desert would take no denial now; and with a shout that rang round the towers of Ardesh, reins were loosed, spears lowered, while, sweeping their bewildered leader onward in their centre, the children of Anak carried all before them in a desperate and irresistible charge.

The brow of Semiramis turned black for very anger, while the beautiful features were distorted with a spasm of rage and scorn.

'The fools!' she hissed between her teeth. 'If but one comes out of the press alive, I will impale him in the centre of the camp! And for their leader —if she be wise, she will die on those Armenian spears, rather than answer this mad frolic in the face of the Great Queen!'

The next moment, with smooth calm smile and

royal dignity, she beckoned Assarac to her chariot, and gave her directions in that calm assured tone which with Semiramis denoted a crisis of extreme peril, and perfect confidence in her own powers to meet it.

What she anticipated did indeed come to pass. The common saying, 'Who shall stand before the children of Anak?' had doubtless grown into a proverb because of its undisputed truth. Individually, the champions of Armenia went down before these stalwart horsemen like corn under the sickle. Iron buckler made no better stand than wicker shield against their mad thrusts and crashing strokes, linked harness proved no stronger fence than linen gown, and bearded men of war seemed but as puny infants contending with this gigantic foe. Charging against the head of the Armenian phalanx, they drove its leaders back upon their fellows; and while they hewed and shouted and smote without remorse, the little band reared about them a barrier of ghastly mutilated corpses, rising to their very girths.

But while thus pressing sore against the front of their enemy, they condensed him into his original formation; and the Great Queen, always intolerant of shortcomings in discipline, had the mortification to witness her well-digested plan destroyed, her whole order of battle put to confusion, by this untoward advance of a force she intended reserving to the last moment for a purpose of her own.

'And ten more spear-lengths would have sufficed,' said she, veiling her vexation as best she might. 'Behold, Assarac! In war, as in peace, it is better to trust a haltered ass than an unbridled steed!'

CHAPTER XII.

LOST AND WON.

SARCHEDON, galloping furiously on his mission, yet cast more than one glance over his shoulder at the battle raging behind him. He too marked the overwhelming charge of the Anakim, and its effect on that solid mass against which its might was hurled. Trained in the subtlest school of war, by the great captain of the age, he perceived at once that if ever they were to be routed, now was the critical moment at which the discomfiture of his countrymen must be achieved. The bay horse reeked with foam and reeled from want of breath when it reached Thorgon's side; and Sarchedon, deeming not an instant should be lost, ventured so far to extend the command he had received as to urge on that old warrior the necessity of putting his men in motion at a gallop. Thorgon frowned and bit his lip. 'Go to!' said he. 'I am not to be taught by an Assyrian youth how to set the battle in array. Nevertheless, if thou wilt share in a death-ride to-day with the children of the north, pull that knife of thine out of thy girdle and come with me.'

Thus speaking, he drew his own long heavy sword, and waving it round his head, placed himself in front of his horsemen, and led them against the enemy at a rapid pace, which, when within a bow-shot distance, he increased to their utmost speed.

The Anakim had now penetrated so far into the ranks of the Armenians as to be nearly surrounded, while victorious, by the very foe they were engaged in defeating. It needed but this charge of Thorgon and his grim long swords in their rear to complete the circle that hemmed them in.

Semiramis, from her chariot, marked the crisis and the manner in which it must be met. 'Assarac,' said she, in her calm modulated voice, 'I cannot trust the children of the desert. They would not retire if I bade them, and so weaken the wedge by drawing it after them in pursuit. We must check these wild cattle of the mountain, nevertheless. Bring up my spears in solid column of a thousand men in front, masking the chariots. When I raise my bow, let them open out and every driver urge his horses to a gallop. I will not give the signal till I see my opportunity, so watch me like a falcon over a fawn. Send for my horsemen clothed in blue. Ten squadrons may serve to bring the Anakim out of peril, and with the rest I will myself make a dash for the person of this Beautiful King.'

Her commands were implicitly obeyed. With a shout that denoted their courage and unshaken confidence, the chief strength of the Assyrian army advanced steadily to the attack.

Meantime the Anakim were fighting at considerable disadvantage. Hemmed in by falling foes, encumbered by dead of their own slaying, they had no space to turn their horses, scarce elbow-room to swing their swords. Twice had Ishtar's rein been seized by a dismounted enemy, and her horse dragged down to its knees; twice had his veiled queen been rescued by some tall champion, who pierced her assailant to the heart, or clove him to the chin. But, nevertheless, the farther these desperate giants fought their way towards the centre of the Armenians, the more difficult became the task of extrication, the more hopeless their chances of retreat. It seemed that all was indeed lost when Thorgon and his long swords came pouring down upon their rear.

To Ishtar the events passing before her eyes were but as the horrors of some ghastly dream. Faint, gasping, terrified, stunned with the din, choked in the dust, blinded by the flash of weapons, sickening at the smell of blood, she was only sensible she had seen Sarchedon, as in a vision, and had cried to him for assistance in vain.

Helpless and bewildered, she must have been slain a score of times but for the chief of the Anakim, whose weapon kept her assailants at bay, while his hand guided her horse through the press of battle; but even this protection failed her when that formidable champion found himself engaged with Thorgon hand to hand.

Wary and experienced, hardened and toughened by continual toil in warfare and the chase, the old Armenian knew every wile of the swordsman, every turn of the horseman, familiarly as he knew the spring of a panther or the rush of a mountain bull. But he was no match for the larger frame and lengthier limbs of an opponent who was a younger, stronger, and quicker man, riding a better horse. While he waved his long sword round his head to cleave his adversary to the girdle, the other smote him sharp and true below the fifth rib, and, with a loud curse on the only god he acknowledged—the weapon that had failed him—Thorgon fell headlong from his saddle, dead before he reached the ground.

Men, horses, flashing weapons, reeling banners—all swam before Ishtar's eyes; and, swaying blindly forward, she was scarcely conscious that a protecting arm supported her, a careful hand guided her bridle, towards the outskirts of the fight.

The fall of their leader seemed in no way to discourage the mountain men; rather they fought with greater fierceness and obstinacy than before. The children of Anak too, considerably outnumbered, and disheartened by the helplessness of their Veiled Queen, began to give way, striking furiously about them indeed, without a thought of flight, yet obviously bent on effecting a retreat, if possible in good order, but at any sacrifice a retreat.

In this imminent crisis of battle, the Comely King and the Great Queen were moved simultaneously with a conviction that now was the moment at which to throw all the weight attainable into the scale. If either side could be driven back but a score of spear-lengths, it might be made to give ground imperceptibly, till wavering grew to flight, and flight culminated in defeat. For Armenia, it seemed the only hope to push forward the wedge till it penetrated and divided the queen's solid columns of spearmen; for the sons of Ashur the sure path to victory lay in a breaking up of that dense obstinate mass, already weakened and mutilated, while its nucleus should be annihilated by their chariots, and its component parts cut to pieces by their horsemen hovering on its flanks.

Therefore Aryas, standing erect in his chariot, encouraged his men of war, with voice and gesture, in the very fore-front of battle. Therefore Semiramis, scanning with undisguised approval the ranks of her body-guard clothed in blue, placed herself joyfully at their head. The Armenian monarch had resolved to save crown, kingdom, and friend, or die, like a true mountain man, in his war-harness; while the Great Queen, thirsting for victory as the drunkard thirsts for wine, was urged by her longing after Sarchedon and the spur of a feminine desire to behold Aryas the Beautiful face to face.

They were now scarce ten spear-lengths apart, on the dried-up river's brink.

The ground was rough and broken, the wheels of

her chariot drove heavily, and Semiramis found herself more than once in danger of being thrown from her elevated position between the horses that plunged and laboured over slippery rock or yielding sand.

Against the carved and inlaid panel beside her hung a quiver with its single arrow—one of those sent to Babylon in return for her embassy, and which she had sworn by Nisroch to plant in the breast of Aryas the Beautiful with her own hand. She snatched it from its case, made a sign to the attendant who led him, leaped on Merodach, and, looking proudly round, raised her bow aloft to brandish it over her head.

Then, while spears went down and bridles shook, a shout rose from the warriors in blue raiment that was caught up by the whole Assyrian army, and every man called lustily on Baal, swearing a mighty oath that he would fight to the death for the Great Queen.

Aiming, as was her custom, at the heart of the enemy, Semiramis broke furiously through the opposing long swords, now deprived of their leader, with the view of first extricating the Anakim from their perilous position, and afterwards directing all her force against the Armenian king in person.

Assarac too had done his part like a practised

warrior. The deep array of spears, a solid column many furlongs in length, strong in its front of a thousand marching men, was nearing the conflict every moment, with that smooth and even step, that mechanical regularity of approach, which seems the very impersonation of discipline and power. Concealed behind its masses, betrayed only by an unceasing jar of iron and roll of wheels, came on those formidable war-chariots, so irresistible by an enemy who had sustained a check that caused the slightest confusion in its ranks; and wielding the whole array, governing at once each element of the storm, drove Assarac the eunuch—he of the cool brain, the steadfast courage, the pitiless heart, who could be moved but by one sentiment on earth—his mad infatuation for the queen.

Aryas marked it all, and knew that now the end was very near. Glancing towards Sarchedon, he beheld his bow-bearer, scarce ten spear-lengths off, in the hottest of the struggle, defending, as it seemed, from stroke and thrust some object at his side. The Anakim gathered about him; while the long swords, shouting, 'Aryas! Aryas!' were making desperate efforts to approach, believing, no doubt, they were rallying round their king.

Semiramis neared her object with every stride. Aryas had stooped to take another arrow from his quiver, and, as he raised his head again to confront his enemy, looking boldly over his shield, behold! for the first time, he stood face to face with the Great Queen.

Deceived by the likeness, duped by her own wild heart and reckless longing, she called on him she loved by the name she had learned to whisper in her dreams; but the hoarse shriek that cried 'Sarchedon, Sarchedon!' was so different from the full soft tones in which she was used to doom a culprit or direct a battle, that her guards pressed fiercely in, thinking their leader must have been stricken with a death-hurt.

Casting down horse and rider in the fury of her career, she urged Merodach towards the chariot, every consideration of war and policy, all care for herself, her army, her people, lost in a fierce thrill of triumph that the desire of her eyes had not escaped her, and she had found him even at the last.

Surrounded by the chosen horsemen of Assyria, over-matched, out-numbered, and now at his sorest need, Aryas shouted to his bow-bearer for help; and Sarchedon, still struggling in the strife as a swimmer fights and reels amongst the breakers, answered lustily to the call.

The Great Queen, making, as she believed, for another, was now within ten paces of Aryas the Beautiful himself.

In that hideous din of battle she neither heard his cry nor the voice that replied to it; but the white horse with the eyes of fire had a truer memory and a sharper ear. Recognising his master's accents, he swerved aside to reach him, but meeting the wrench of the queen's practised hand on his bridle, reared high with tossing head, and plunging blindly forward against the king's chariot, struck himself and his rider heavily to the ground.

As the good horse rolled over a maimed Armenian, the dying mountain man shortened the sword he grasped fiercely even then, and buried it in the animal's bowels.

Agile as a panther, Semiramis extricated herself, and was up like lightning; but when she saw the beast she prized so dearly dead at her very feet, her heart burned, and her eyes blazed with a fury wilder, fiercer, madder, than the rage of any beast of prey.

Baffled, stunned, bewildered, she only knew that Merodach lay slain beneath her; that an armed enemy stood above with shielded face and javelin raised to strike; that here across the body of her horse was the turning-point of battle, and that she held a bow and arrow in her hand. Unconsciously, she fitted the one to the string, and drew the other at a venture, as it were, in self-defence.

It was the Armenian arrow, cut in Armenian forests, tipped with Armenian steel. It had travelled to Babylon and back as a symbol of dignified remonstrance and royal self-respect; now the white cruel arm impelled it straight and true, to find its home in the heart of an Armenian king.

Stricken below the buckler, he felt his life-blood oozing down to wet its feathers, drop by drop.

'Turn thy hand out of the battle,' murmured Aryas to his charioteer, 'since I am hurt even unto death!'

But he never spoke again; for the Great Queen's men of war, making in to aid their leader, hurled him from his chariot, gashing with pitiless sword-strokes the comely face so fair even in death, crushing under trampling hoofs the stately form that, maimed, bruised, and mangled, was grand and kingly still.

So the horsemen of Assyria triumphed; her spears made victory secure, her chariots rolled over the slain. The blue mantles smote and spared not; the Anakim, extricating themselves, not without considerable loss, departed in good order; and the pursuit rolled on till the sons of Ashur sacked the town of Ardesh—to burn, pillage, and destroy, even unto the going down of the day.

But men looked in vain for her who had led the attack and achieved the victory, asking each other with eager looks and anxious faces,

'What tidings of the Great Queen?'

Her armour lay, piece by piece, beside her; there was dust on her lustrous hair, the pride of her royal garment was rent from hem to hem, while bowed down in anguish, with fixed eyes, white face, and rigid lips, she knelt beside a dead horse, over the body of a dead king.

CHAPTER XIII.

SHARING THE SPOIL.

In the palace of Ardesh, where the naked sword stood for men to worship, they set up a golden image of Baal; where a free monarch sat amongst his free warriors, the servant of a despotic mistress now lorded it over a conquered race. Between rise and set of sun a king had perished, an army had been cut to pieces, and a warlike people ceased to hold its place among nations.

In the court of that royal dwelling, under the soft evening sky, Assarac stood in state to receive the captains of the host, take note of their prisoners, and count the spoil. He had borne him all day like a warrior of might—cool as the wariest of leaders, bold as the fiercest of spearmen. None the less was his practised eye scanning the material results of triumph, his active brain plotting to consolidate the fruits of victory.

Though himself unwounded, the eunuch's harness was riven and dented, the linen garment, which, in right of his priestly office, he affected even in battle, was streaked and spotted with blood. Fed by the fire within, his look was keen and piercing; there seemed little more trace of fatigue on his care-worn face than it had worn day and night since the host marched out from the northern gate of Babylon; and, conscious he had borne him like a true son of Ashur, under the eyes of the Great Queen, his aspect, lately so dejected and morose, was brightened by a passing gleam, as from the light of hope.

It looked a ghastly task on which his mind was bent. Files of Assyrian spearmen, passing proudly before him, laid down the heads of enemies slain in arms or taken prisoners after the combat; so lavishly and with such precision, that a pile of these hideous trophies had already risen to the height of a man's girdle. Two scribes, tablet in hand, took note of their exact number; while Assarac, as the queen's chief counsellor, recorded the names of the successful warriors, and apportioned the share to which each would be entitled in dividing the spoil.

Not a murmur rose against his award; for it was still fresh in men's minds how at the turning-point of battle, when victory hung doubtful in the balance, all that fierce energy and daring which had rendered Ninus such a successful leader seemed to have descended on the priest of Baal whom the old king so mistrusted and reviled.

Man by man the champions of the Assyrian host passed by. One laden with the spoil he had already gathered, rude in workmanship, yet precious in its barbaric splendour and intrinsic worth. Another, dragging some hapless foeman, whom he had bound securely with his girdle, and whose fate hung on the eunuch's nod; for the conqueror, with bared arm and naked steel, held himself ready to pierce, flay, or decapitate at the lightest sign. A third, leading a comely mountain maid, white and ruddy, with shy blue eyes and tangled locks of gold, scared, trembling, weeping, yet sometimes blushing, not without conscious triumph, that she had herself taken captive the strong fighter in whose power she seemed to be.

For the vanquished, Assarac now showed a clemency unusual in the traditions of his people, not entirely in accordance with his own nature, as it had hitherto appeared, hard, practical, uninfluenced by feeling, and looking only to results. It was observed, that he spared all captives save only such warriors as had been taken fighting against the body-guards of the Great Queen; while for the Armenian women, in this their hour of sorrow, he manifested a pity and consideration that elicited certain ribald comments from his countrymen, and no small surprise from the prisoners themselves. But censure, praise, and ridicule were alike unable to affect him to-day. With that power of concentration which constitutes the principal element of success in war, government, or indeed any business of life, his energies were engrossed in the important task of so disposing that great Assyrian army, as to provide for security and good order in the captured town.

Leader after leader therefore he summoned and dismissed, receiving their tale of spoil and captives, giving directions for the distribution of their men. 'Where has he learned his skill of warfare,' said the old captains to each other, 'this high-priest of our Assyrian god? Surely Baal comes down to him by night and speaks with him face to face.'

So strongly was national pride and self-confidence imbued with a religious belief in their gods, that this opinion seemed to the sons of Ashur extremely probable and well-conceived. It reflected honour on themselves, their worship, and their triumph; above all, it invested Assarac with an influence and authority most essential in the absence of the Great Queen. Not a line of the eunuch's face, not a turn of his body, was permitted to weaken this impression of superhuman strength and sagacity, of holiness fresh from the fount of fire itself. Calm, dignified, imperious, moved by no casualty, equal to all occasions, he issued his commands with a foresight and wisdom that elicited order from the very excesses of a victorious army in a city taken by assault; and yet at Assarac's heart, though stifled and suppressed by the strong will within, raged a tumult far more difficult to deal with in its unbridled folly than the wildest license of warriors drunk with wine and blood.

Where was the queen? Again and again had that question presented itself in the hour of victory, and now, though the stars were out, he could not answer it yet.

While driving the Armenians back upon the town of Ardesh, and entering their capital with a routed enemy, he never doubted but that Semiramis was performing her part of the battle, and that they would meet at sunset in the Comely King's palace, where he would receive from her some acknowledgment of the valour he had shown, some word of thanks for the service he had done. For a time the exigencies of such a success left him not a moment to make inquiries concerning the mistress of nations, even had it been prudent to do so. It was necessary to assume supreme authority, and wield it without scruple; but when a clear head, an undisputed will, and an unequalled organisation had disposed of their immediate necessities, and the Assyrian host with its captives was securely established for the night, Assarac's anxiety became maddening as hour by hour passed on, but brought no tidings of the Great Queen.

It never entered his head that she could be slain. To him, Ashtaroth was no more an impersonation of light, beauty, and unearthly power than Semiramis. That she might have been taken up at the moment of victory, to join the stars of heaven in a chariot of fire, he was perhaps the only man of all the host who did *not* believe; but none the less was it impossible for him to realise that imperial glory as shadowed by defeat, that matchless face as pale and fixed in death.

Thus was he spared more than one hideous pang;

yet perhaps it is a question whether the suspense that racked him now, with all its maddening possibilities, was not fiercer torture than would have been the certainty that she was gone from him for ever, and he must grovel before his idol no more.

While the stars shone coldly down on the scene of conflict, while a new moon shed her gentle light on fire-scathed tower and blackened wall above — on writhing sufferer and stiffened corpse below — on riven harness, prostrate horses, chariots broken where they fell — on the tents of the conquerors, the lines of the vanquished, the wounded, the sleeping, the dying, and the great banner of Ashur drooping sullenly over all, — Assarac wrapped himself in a dark-coloured mantle, and leaving the royal palace of Ardesh, stole down to the plain below, hoping that on the field of battle, where he had last seen her, he might recover some traces of the queen.

Already, ere he proceeded half a bow-shot, he had disturbed a jackal at its loathsome feast. The eunuch shuddered and hurried on. Was this, then, the end and climax of all the pomp of war, the glory of the host, the thunder of chariots, the shouting of captains, the sword, the shield, and the battle?

A nation rising in its might at sunrise, going

forth to conquer, and at nightfall—lo, a wild dog mumbling a bone!

His pursuits, his profession, the juggleries that deceived the people, the pseudo-science that professed to read the stars, had taught him, perhaps, to ponder and reflect, where others of his nation were content to act and to enjoy. Looking from the scene of carnage at his feet to that summer's night so fair and pure above, the great question thrust itself upon his mind, which his experience, his reason, all the traditions of Ashur, all the mystic lore of Baal, seemed unable to answer.

What was this confusion on earth, this order and regularity in heaven, and why were these things so? Did Nisroch take thought for that Armenian woman, wailing in the darkness over the body of her dead lord, or Baal pity the maimed swordsman yonder, trailing his length like a crushed reptile towards the stream that, in his agony of thirst, he forgot had been drained and turned aside? Was there indeed a motive power to govern in heaven? And if so, did it leave the evils of earth to right themselves as best they might, by force, fraud, and subtlety, the strong arm and the cunning brain? A thrill of triumph passed through him, while he murmured,

'It must be so! Let him lord it up yonder who will, man is the god below; and he who never flinches from his purpose shall not fail in his desire. Such a one stands here to-night in these my garments. Conqueror of the north, Assarac the eunuch has to-day taken his place among the mighty ones of earth, and who shall say him nay? Hath he not led the hosts of Assyria to victory? Hath he not adjudged to each triumphant man of war the meed of his deserts; and shall not he also take his share of the spoil? Costly jewels, treasures of gold, herds of camels, horses, armour, and cunning needle-work—the common needs of common men—he careth for none of these; and yet to-night, surely to-night, shall he garner the harvest that has been sown in fire, and reaped in blood. Ashtaroth, Ashtaroth, queen of love and light, hast thou ever known a worshipper who flung before thee all he had to give, taking his heart out, to lay it at thy feet, and asked only in return for one approving glance, one soft and kindly smile? Surely she to whom I pray cannot withhold these from me in such a time as this! Surely there is a goodly meed in store for him who has to-day placed her crowning victory on the brows of the Great Queen!'

He had nearly reached the river's bed, where the battle had been hottest, where the carnage lay thick and reeking in broad swathes of slaughter; a few more steps brought him to where Merodach lay stiff and cold, with a vulture feasting on his eyes, and a wild dog tearing at his flank. The bright stars and the young moon afforded light enough to distinguish the dead white horse with its ghastly attendants. Assarac's brain reeled, his blood ran cold, while he remembered that he had last seen its rider charging furiously through the battle, on the back of her favourite.

The vulture croaked and flapped its wings, the wild dog growled, glared, and slunk away. Like a man chained in a nightmare, half conscious that he is dreaming, yet wholly unable to resist the petrifying spell, Assarac felt as if some unseen power compelled him to remain and confront the nameless horror that he so dreaded, yet was so resolved to disbelieve. He tried to shout, but his tongue clave to the roof of his mouth; to draw his sword, but his hand hung powerless, and his flesh crept, so that the very hair rose in the nape of his neck; for gliding through the gloom, scarce half a bow-shot off, there passed him a ghostly procession, such as the spirits of the dead might form, in their land of shadows beyond the grave.

Four tall dark figures, moving with solemn gait, bore aloft, on one of the long wicker shields used by assailants of a fenced city, such a shrouded burden as denoted the presence of death under the cloak that veiled its ghastly truth.

Behind them, with drooping head, clasped hands, and a bearing that betrayed the utmost abandonment of woe, walked a female mourner, majestic even in the hour of sorrow that bowed her to the earth. Assarac started into life now, if indeed that could be called life which was but restoration to consciousness under the smart of a deadly stab; for in the folds hanging about the corpse he recognised a royal mantle—in the drooping and dejected mourner, beheld the person of the Great Queen.

With fixed and rigid face, with hands clasped tight, with steps that seemed borne up and guided by some extraneous power, independent of and even dominating his own will, the eunuch followed through the darkness, as a sleep-walker follows the immaterial object of his dreams, never decreasing the space that intervened, never turning aside from the foot-prints of those who led, passing without heed over mailed corpse and broken chariot, through sand and shingle and shallow pools of blood.

So the procession laboured gravely on, away from the battle-field, across the vineyards, up the rocky path that led to those mountain forests in which the dead king of Armenia might have found safety from his foes.

The bearers neither increased their speed nor halted, nor stinted for lack of breath, but moved calmly forward with even measured pace, symbol of a haughty reverence and respect, rather than of pity or distress; for he whom they bore feet foremost had been a warrior like themselves, and lay warlike in his riven harness, with a broken bow in his hand. He had fallen, as was meet for a stout champion, in the fore-front of battle, and though the horsemen of Assyria slashed it cruelly with their swords, his comely face had never turned one hair's-breadth from the foe.

Therefore the sons of Ashur thought no shame to carry him sternly and proudly to his rest, at the command of their mistress; therefore in their hearts they told themselves, how at Nisroch's appointed time, it would be well for them too that they should die in their armour, and that their last end should be like his.

The frogs clamoured in the marsh, the night wind moaned in the pines, filmy clouds swept over the crescent moon, and the corpse went ever upward into the mountain, while the queen followed after it, weeping, mute, unconscious, and Assarac, giddy and bewildered, followed blindly after the queen.

CHAPTER XIV.

COUNTING THE COST.

EVER as their path grew steeper, and they penetrated farther into its recesses, the forest became more gloomy, while its trees assumed more hideous and fantastic shapes. The sky was dark and wild, the air loaded with those murmurs of the night that are to sounds of waking life as passing shadows to real objects of flesh and blood; gigantic faces, grim, gray, and indistinct, blinked and peered from naked crag or gnarled and wrinkled trunk; while here, there, everywhere around, brooded a presence, no less awful because so vague and impalpable, that would have curdled and chilled the boldest human heart. It seemed to Assarac, he was treading the border-land between here and hereafter; that at every step he might come face to face with some departed spirit, for which the universal experience was no longer a problem to be solved, which could tell him the secret all his life had been but an effort to inquire.

A white owl flitted noiselessly through the darkness, and the eunuch's heart stood still with something less debasing, yet far more horrible than fear. Nevertheless, as the shadowy train moved before him, mechanically he followed on.

In a gorge of the mountain, where night was blackest, a red light glowed suddenly across the sky. Wheeling round the stem of a rugged oak, the bearers halted with their burden, in an open space where four glades met, converging on an indistinct mass, that seemed, in the fitful glare, some rough rude altar reared of unhewn stones.

Reverently they laid the dead hero down. Rising erect, when he touched the earth, Assarac recognised in their lofty frames and costly armour four spearmen from the body-guard of the Great Queen.

Semiramis stood apart, peering eagerly into the gloom, only the outline of a white face visible in the deep folds of a mantle, that shrouded her head and figure.

Wild yells and piercing shrieks rose from the forest, while the flash of many torches danced fitfully among the trees. A score of hideous figures now came leaping into the open space, and formed themselves in a circle round the queen, the spearmen, and the dead warrior laid upon his shield.

Interest and curiosity had somewhat mastered the eunuch's over-powering sense of horror, so that waking, as it were, from the oppression of a trance, he seemed to resume his faculties of body and mind.

He knew the shapes at last, recognising them for those frantic votaries who, electing to worship Abitur of the Mountains, disowned all human ties and interests, abjured all other creeds and professions, that they might serve the great principle of evil in the wilderness.

These men were naked to the waist, their hair and beards were matted and tangled in foul disorder, they tossed their lean arms aloft with frantic vehemence, and their eyes glared in the torchlight with the fierce cunning of insanity.

They might have been themselves the demons they adored, so strange and unearthly was their appearance, while dancing, gibbering, howling, they came and went, now opening out, now closing in, their circle, now retiring among the trees, now advancing towards the altar, but still, like vultures about a carrion, converging gradually round the corpse.

The queen held up her hand; immediately the torches gave a steadier light, the wavering shapes were still, and prostrated themselves before her with mute signs of submission, reverence, even abject fear.

She had protected the sect, respected their tenets, even joined in their worship, from motives of policy long ago.

Now, in her great need, she clung to this desperate resource, and had come to wring from Abitur of the Mountains that which the host of heaven seemed unable to bestow.

With the increased light afforded by a score of torches, no longer whirled and brandished in the air, Assarac observed that, in the rock over against him, was hewn an entrance to some vast cavernous temple, ornamented with rough symbols and grotesque representations of the demon worshipped within. This cavity seemed partly natural, partly hollowed out from the bowels of the earth, by the same rude labour that had erected the altar in its front.

Four of the wild men raised the burden recently laid down by the Assyrian warriors, and, preceded by two of their companions with torches, disappeared in the entrance of the temple or mouth of the cavern. While they lifted the corpse, Semiramis passed her hand, with a gesture of exceeding tenderness, over the dead face, and followed close behind, succeeded by the rest of the torch-bearing troop, leaving the spearmen without, as if to guard the threshold.

An irresistible impulse drove the eunuch onward in his strange adventure, yet it seemed that he could not have uttered a word to save his life. With every faculty strained, every sense painfully sharpened, speech was alone denied him.

The sons of Ashur crossed their spears to bar his entrance; but throwing the cloak back from his face, though still without a word, he caused them to recognise him that stood at the right hand of the Great Queen, and thus passed unimpeded into the temple of the fiend.

In a vaulted cavern, so lofty that the glare of twenty torches scarce illumined the shadowy masses of its roof, stood four unhewn blocks of granite, supporting, at the height of a man's knee, a rough slab of the same, on a flooring of rock, over which nature had spread a deep covering of sand. There was here no appearance of shrine or altar, none of those attempts at ornament, by which even the rudest of worshippers do honour to their deity with hand and brain. The walls of this natural temple were of bare bulging stone, its roof was reared far into the bowels of the mountain; it had but one aperture, through which a dim thread of light might be seen at noonday, and where, if he ever did visit them, the worshippers of Abitur were taught to expect the appearance of their master.

Buried in the depths of the forest, beneath those wild shaggy hills, this dwelling of the evil principle was as dark and shadowy, compared with the temple of Baal, as that shrine of the Assyrian god, glowing in vermilion and gold, seemed poor and paltry to the starry dome above, of which it professed to be the type.

From behind a jutting boulder of rock, forming, as it were, a natural buttress of the cavern, Assarac watched in horror. The dew stood on his brow, damp and chill as the slime on the surface against which he leaned.

Semiramis snatched a torch from one of the wild figures at her side, and with its unlighted end described a triangular figure, while keeping herself carefully within that mystic border, around the broad flat stone on which the dead man lay.

A wild unreasoning terror then seemed to take possession of the worshippers, they trembled from head to foot, and cowered back as far as the limits of the cavern would allow. In the silence that succeeded this movement, even Assarac expected some tangible horror to appear.

The Great Queen planted her torch firmly in the sand at the corpse's head, stripping off at the same time its enshrouding mantle, while her own cloak fell from her shoulders in the act, revealing at one stroke her matchless beauty and the glittering splendour of her attire.

It was a ghastly contrast—the same wavering light that played on the queen's jewels imparted a flicker of life and motion to the dead man's face, gashed and seamed with the sword, drawn and distorted with spasms of mortal pain. He seemed to gasp, to gibber, to be about to speak, as if the longing eyes that looked down on him were indeed able to draw his very soul back from those unknown regions to which it had taken flight, as if the force of a woman's will, the desire of a woman's love, must needs have power to bridge the gulf that parts the living and the dead.

Was it indeed Sarchedon who lay there disfigured

into so maimed and unsightly an object? And did she love him so dearly, that now to-night, in the very hour of her triumph, she could forego her royal pomp and glory, could stoop her neck and bend her pride for such a thing as this?

Then Assarac felt at his heart that keen and searching stab to which every other pain is but as a dull outward bruise to a serpent's venomed sting.

With dropped jaw, fixed eyes, and rigid limbs, he watched like a man turned to stone.

She plucked an amulet from her neck, gazing on it for an instant ere she laid it softly, tenderly, in the dead man's breast. Then she looked upward, moving lips and hands, like one who pleads hard for life, though not a sound came forth. This was the second time she had bartered away her mystic charm. Surely all her resources of peace and war must stand her in some stead! Surely the dove and the arrow would not fail her now!

When she turned her eyes again to the body, they gleamed with the light of hope. On her face was the smile that welcomes some dear one's home-coming, and she stretched her arms, as if to invite the wanderer back to her loving heart.

But while still he moved not, lying there stark

and rigid, without word or sign, it seemed strange to Assarac, that the Great Queen, whose nature was so imperious, manifested neither anger nor impatience at this protracted opposition to her will. Sorrow indeed came down over the beautiful face like a veil; but through it there shone the exceeding tenderness of a love that owns no limit of time or place, that acknowledges no barrier, even in the chasm of an open grave.

Once more her lips and eyes moved wildly, once more she looked around, as if to plead for that fiendish help she had come here to implore; then while her bosom heaved, and her throat swelled high, she burst into a strain of melody that rang through the remotest corners of the cavern, causing the wild men's senses to thrill with a strange intoxicating delight, and the eunuch's heart to quiver with a fierce intolerable pain.

It was the incantation by which, in sight of all the gods of her people, she protested against her loss, calling on the parted spirit to return from its place beyond the grave.

Laying her right hand on the dead man's forehead, her left upon his heart, she raised her head and sang:

By the power of the Seven
    Great tokens of light;
By the Judges of Heaven,
    The watchers of night;
By the might of those forces
    That govern on high,
The Stars in their courses,
    The hosts of the sky;
By Ashur, grim pagan,
    Our father in mail;
By Nebo and Dagon,
    By Nisroch and Baal;
By pale Ishtar, contrasting
    With red Merodach,
By the wings everlasting,
    I summon thee back!

From the ranks of a legion
    That files through the gloom
Of a shadowy region
    Disclosed by the tomb;
From the gulf of black sorrow
    Of silence and sleep,
Where a night with no morrow
    Broods over the deep;
By desire unavailing,
    And pleasure that's fled;
By the living bewailing
    Her love for the dead;
By the wish that endears thee,
    The kisses that burn,
And the passion that sears thee,
    I bid thee return!

Thou art cold, and thy face is
    So waxen at rest,
In my fiery embraces
    Seek warmth on my breast.

> Through the lips that caress thee
>   Draw balm in my breath,
> And the arms that compress thee
>   Shall wrench thee from Death.
> Though he boasteth to spare not
>   For ransom or fee,
> Yet he shall not, he dare not,
>   Take tribute of me.
> Then if love can restore thee,
>   Though bound on the track,
> From the journey before thee,
>   Belovèd, come back!'

While the last syllables died on her lips in long pathetic tones, she sank across the dead body, brow to brow, breast to breast, and mouth to mouth. Surely, if but one spark of life had been left, that wild embrace must have drawn and kindled it into flame.

But Assarac's brain reeled, and the cavern swam before his eyes. Staggering, suffocated, he hastened from the place, passing the men of war at the entrance as he rushed blindly out into the darkness. Said one spearman to his comrade, 'Surely it is a spirit. Behold how it vanisheth in the night!' To which the other, leaning thoughtfully on his shield, replied,

'It is the demon who hath entered, and taken possession of the man, and driven him forth, and fled with him into the wilderness.'

CHAPTER XV.

THE VOICE OF THE CHARMER.

It was not the custom of an Assyrian army to leave its work half done. The day after the great battle of Ardesh, the Armenians were scattered to the four winds of heaven. Thorgon and his long swords indeed lay on the field in regular lines of rank and file, as they had fallen; but, though resisting bravely while his crest could be seen above the tumult, when their king went down, the remnant of the mountain men broke up and fled in confusion to their homes. The very stratagem that had, as it were, doubled his presence for their encouragement, served perhaps but to dishearten them the more, when they no longer beheld the royal form which had hitherto seemed ubiquitous in the fight. Every portion of his host was satisfied it had taken its orders directly from the monarch; and when at last those two mailed figures, each of which was believed to be Aryas himself, came together in the hottest of the conflict, men lay so thick about the spot, that few indeed were left to observe the fall of one and disappearance of the other warrior, either of whom might have been their king.

Through many a league of mountain pass and tangled brake, fording the torrent or scouring the wind-swept plain, fled broken bands of fugitives, panting, scared, disarmed, looking wildly over their shoulders for the fierce and terrible foe, who spared not where he conquered, and when he lifted sword or javelin, never failed to drive it home.

But there was one troop of horsemen, scanty in number, yet formidable in appearance, that although fighting on the side of victory had suffered considerable loss. Returning towards the south in fair and orderly retreat, it yet bore no symptoms of discomfiture or flight. The children of Anak presented rather the appearance of assailants proceeding on some promising expedition than of a solitary force wilfully deserting the cause it had espoused. They restrained their invincible little hōrses to a steady regulated pace, halting at frequent intervals to show a bold front in case of pursuit from friend or foe. Their arms were bright, and held in readiness; their bearing was haughty and full of confidence; even the wounded sat firm and upright in their saddles, and at any moment all seemed prepared to resume the fray.

In the centre rode their Veiled Queen, accompanied by one in Armenian armour, who seemed less a prisoner than a guest.

While the battle raged at its fiercest round the white stone which Semiramis had marked as its turning-point, Ishtar found herself carried on its tide against the very person of him whom she had come to seek. It needed but a wave of her arm to rally round her those champions who believed so simply in her supernatural attributes, with whom no horsemen in the world could counter stroke for stroke. Pressing in on their leader, they soon encircled Ishtar and Sarchedon, soon cut their way to the outskirts of the battle, and merging alike their compact with Semiramis and their own love of fighting in blind obedience to their queen, drew off in perfectly good order, to commence a steady retreat for their southern home.

The Assyrian had seen Aryas fall in fight, had noted the destruction of the long swords, the total rout of those hardy warriors who hoped in vain to make head against his countrymen. What was left him now, but to drift with the stream of fate in the arms of the woman he loved?

The Anakim soon recognised him as the companion of their leader, when first she appeared among their tents and they knew her not. This was enough to insure their protection and regard. At the first halt, there was even a question of receiving him as an adopted brother in the tribe; but he wanted more than a span of the necessary stature, and that project was unwillingly abandoned. Nevertheless, every man felt pledged to do him homage and defend his person to the death.

It seemed to Sarchedon that he was riding through some unreal paradise in a dream. He told Ishtar as much, while she related her trials, her sorrows, and her undeviating constancy since they parted in the desert after their flight from Ascalon. He feared to wake, he said, and find himself again in that Egyptian dungeon, from which escape seemed hopeless as from the tomb.

'Beloved,' she answered, 'the queen of heaven will not permit us to be tried yet farther. Behold! twice has she brought you deliverance through me her servant in your hour of greatest need. It is enough. We shall be parted no more. We will cast in our lot with these children of the wilderness: they are brave, generous, faithful; they will fence us from our enemies with a hedge of steel.'

'Be it so,' he answered, looking fondly in the dear face that was unveiled only to *him*. 'Better a goats' hair tent with Ishtar in the desert than a painted chamber and an empty heart in the palace of a king. And yet,' he added somewhat wistfully, 'I would fain see the inside of great Babylon again before I die.'

They were crossing a fair and level plain, the mountains above Ardesh were already sinking on the horizon, and the children of the desert welcomed that smooth unvaried surface, as reminding them of the boundless tract they called their home.

Presently the chief, riding warily in their rear, shouted to halt. Forming towards the point of danger, they observed a column of dust rising in the distance, as of an armed party proceeding rapidly on their track.

To those observant eyes, prompt and reliable information was afforded by the lightest tokens of earth or sky. While Sarchedon could detect but a rolling yellow cloud, the sons of Anak told each other of ten score horsemen and a war-chariot travelling at speed.

They bore down, therefore, in the direction of the approaching party, forming carefully round Ishtar and her companion in case of conflict.

When within a furlong of each other, both troops somewhat slackened pace, and a chariot, driven furiously towards the Anakim, was stopped at a spear-length from their chief.

Standing in it, erect and fearless before drawn bows and levelled spears, with head bared, shield lowered in token of amity, Assarac raised his unarmed hands, and cried in a loud voice, 'Is it peace, O my brother?'

'Let there be peace, my brother, between thee and me,' answered the chief of the Anakim; and the eunuch, getting down out of his chariot, proceeded to explain the reason of his coming and his absence in the hour of victory from the army of the Great Queen.

'Semiramis,' he said, 'had been grievously wounded at the very moment of triumph. If not hurt to the death, she was at least unable to retain command of the host, or even to provide for the government of her empire at home. Therefore must he hasten back to Babylon, that he might rule wisely and in accordance with the laws of Shinar, while the queen's authority was thus for a space in abeyance. New times were coming—a new policy, perhaps a new dominion. Those who were so skilful to rein a steed and wield a sword must ever be welcome to a warlike government, such as could alone control the sons of Ashur. He had it in his power to offer the Anakim a tract of fertile country, a land of corn and wine and oil, in which to dwell at ease, ruled by their hereditary chief and subject to their fathers' laws. Would they not hold it of the Great Queen by service of bow and spear, each man sitting under his own vine and his own fig-tree, doing that which seemed good in his own eyes?'

The Anakim glanced doubtfully at each other; their chief pointed to the mare from which he had dismounted, and shook his head.

'I could not breathe Lotus-flower,' said he, 'in the confines of such a tract. Like the wild ass, whose speed she laughs to scorn, her limbs would stiffen if she might not stretch them on a plain boundless as the sky that meets it on every side.'

'There is rich spoil to share,' urged the eunuch. 'Herds of sheep, oxen, and camels, droves of captives — men, women, and children — wine, jewels, goodly raiment, and gold to be had for the asking.'

The other stooped his tall person to bend his bow against the hollow of his foot and ease its string.

'All these,' he answered, 'I can have by the tightening of this weapon in my hand. What need I more than the inheritance of my fathers—the desert sun, the trackless sand, and the goods of every man whose spear is a span shorter than mine own? Go to, thou lordly son of Ashur! my portion is better than thine. I have spoken. Take a gift from thy servant, and depart in peace.'

Assarac would never have been in his present position had he admitted the impossibility of an enterprise because of its first failure.

'I will accept the gift of my brother,' said he, receiving with exceeding courtesy a loaf of barley-bread and a handful of dried dates, offered by one of the Anakim at a signal from his chief. 'May it be returned to him a hundredfold when he encamps without the gate of Babylon, and I, even I, Assarac, governor of the city, bow my head at the door of his tent to do him honour! If we may not draw bow again side by side in battle, at least let there be peace between thy people and my people, so that a son of Ashur, meeting a child of Anak in the wilderness, shall cast his spear down before him and say, Is it well with thee, O my brother?'

Pausing to mark the effect of these friendly sentiments, and observing that they were well received by his listeners, the eunuch turned to Sarchedon, and continued in a lighter tone:

'There is indeed a new dominion in Babylon when those laws of the land of Shinar have been set aside which sentence to death that Assyrian-born who shall be found arrayed in war-harness against the banner of Ashur. And therefore, Sarchedon, if thou art a prisoner amongst these my brethren, I will ransom thee at a royal price. If a friend, I will bid thee leave them for a space, to their profit and thine own. If a captain and leader, I will promote thee to yet higher honour in the great army that has never known defeat.'

Sarchedon, glancing doubtfully at Ishtar, noted the colour fade from her cheek ere she drew the veil over her face. Nevertheless, the tempter was skilled in his art; and the prospect of once more bearing arms with his countrymen was too welcome to be dismissed.

'I would fain return to the land of my fathers,'

said he, 'and ride to battle with my brethren in burnished armour and costly raiment once more. But yet it is better to dwell in the desert with a whole skin than to writhe on a stake in the sun, even though it be over against the palace of a king. If I came in the light of the Great Queen's countenance, behold, she would consume me in her wrath. If Ninyas reigned in her stead, my death might peradventure be more merciful, but more speedy also, and no less sure.'

Assarac had a purpose to serve, and the lie glided smooth and facile from his lips.

'Semiramis,' he answered—and even now, in this his hour of fierce revenge and mad disloyalty, he could not speak that name without a quiver of the lip, a tremble of the voice—'Semiramis sickens in her tent with a death-hurt. Ninyas her son, sunk in sloth and pleasure, lover of the garland, the wine-cup, and the couch, would soon weary of the sceptre as he wearied of the sword. The Assyrian ruler needs a wise brain and a long arm. The Assyrian people look for qualities in their kings that are the attributes of their gods. Ninus will never return to us from the stars; but Ninus was less powerful than Nimrod, even as Nimrod himself was weaker than Ashur, from whose loins he sprang. Why should we, his descendants, owe allegiance to any earthly power? Why should kings, queens, and princes come between Baal and the people of his choice?'

The audacious project of wresting from the line of Nimrod that dynasty it had held with so strong a hand, and substituting a hierarchy of which he should himself be the head, had long appeared to Assarac a feasible project enough—one worthy of his own tameless energy and insatiable ambition, although the temptation had been stifled hitherto by his loyalty, his devotion to the queen. Now, in the torture of a vexed heart and wounded spirit, he swore to cast aside every sentiment but revenge, at least till Semiramis was at the mercy of him whose fidelity she had used, and scorned, and outraged without remorse. Therefore, it would be well, he thought, to strengthen his hands with all the weapons he could seize, to make such friends for himself on every side as should become willing tools, to ply at need, and cast away at will. When he met them by chance in the plain, it struck him that the Anakim would be no contemptible auxiliaries; when he found Ishtar and Sarchedon in their midst, he reflected that the former might still be made a bait, if necessary, for the allurement of Ninyas; the latter, according as events fell out, might form a snare, a bribe, or a punishment for the Great Queen. That she believed him to have been killed, and in her agony of sorrow thought to raise him from the dead, he knew by the evidence of his own senses, and although the Armenian habit, in which he now recognised Sarchedon, convinced him of her error, the bitterness of his anguish seemed rather enhanced than modified by this discovery that the object of her desire was not yet wholly out of reach.

It was scarcely jealousy he experienced, for jealousy implies possession, past, present, or prospective; it was rather that morbid recklessness of despair, which pulls down the whole edifice on its own head, if only the idol may be crushed and buried in the ruins of its shrine.

Could he have hated her as sincerely as he wished, he would, perhaps, have triumphed, and, favoured by circumstances, might have held the proud Semiramis in his power, if only for a day; but when did man ever succeed in any perilous enterprise who suffered his heart to paralyse his arm, the outcry of his affections to drown the promptings of his brain?

Nevertheless, it was his present object to gain

over Sarchedon, and after a pause, as of deep consideration, he spoke out with a semblance of the utmost frankness :

'Hearken, my son. Let nothing be kept back between thee and me. Baal, though he lead a host in heaven, needs also an army here on earth. That army must have a captain. He who has set the battle in array for friend and foe, at home, in Egypt, here among the mountains of the north, is surely well fitted to command the warriors of the Assyrian god. When Assarac declares his will from the altar before his temple at home, Sarchedon shall stand forth in shining raiment, chief and Tartan of the great Assyrian host. Said I well, my son? and wilt thou not follow me in all haste to Babylon?'

He had bought him, he thought, for a price, and, through him, that foolish girl, together with this formidable tribe of stalwart simple-minded warriors.

Again Sarchedon glanced at Ishtar; but her veil was down, and she made no sign.

'To lead the host!' he muttered thoughtfully. 'To have the power of Ninus, and wield it wisely, as did Arbaces!'

'Ponder it well, my son,' said the eunuch solemnly, 'while I speed on to prepare the way.

What art thou here?' he added, lowering his voice. 'A hostage in a foeman's camp, at a woman's will. Behold, I can make thee the noblest leader on earth, and she, this veiled queen of a handful of horsemen, shall sit on the throne of a province larger than the great northern land we went out to conquer. What Baal offers, do not thou despise. Go to! Stretch forth thy hand, and take it whilst thou canst. To-morrow it may be too late. I have spoken.'

Then, with a courteous farewell to the Anakim, he mounted into his chariot, and was gone, speeding, like some pestilent wind, towards the south on his mission of treachery, rebellion, and revenge.

CHAPTER XVI.

REQUITED.

'I HAVE cast stones in the air to fall on mine own head! I have knelt at the stream, and, lo, the waters were bitter and defiled! O Kalmim, there is neither faith, nor honour, nor gratitude in Ninyas, the son of Ninus. May the king live for ever!'

She laughed outright. It was a rare jest to behold Sethos in a vein of serious reflection; above all, to hear him revile the prince to whom, through good and evil, he had been a devoted servant, notwithstanding the vices, caprices, and heartless ingratitude of his lord.

'You are but a child,' she answered lightly, 'and for all your downy lip and shapely limbs, not yet fit to run alone. Trust a strained bow, a frayed string, a blown horse, or a baffled woman—all these will quit them better in the hour of need than a king on the throne, whom you have served when he was a captive in the dungeon.'

They were standing together on a terrace of the royal palace in Babylon, looking over many a league of gardens, vineyards, lofty palms, thin silvery streams — vast tracts of desert sand beyond — all shining and glowing in the bright morning sun, while their own comely faces and splendid attire were rich and deep in colour as the surrounding hues of earth and sky.

A great change had indeed taken place at home, since the queen's expedition to Armenia left the city without a ruler, while its lawful prince languished a weary prisoner, losing health, energy, and all the dignity of manhood, under supervision of the priests of Baal. The return of Assarac, bearing, as he affirmed, full powers and authority on the part of Semiramis, sickening even to death in the far north, had extricated Ninyas from captivity, and placed him on the throne to which he was entitled by the laws of Shinar, the eunuch, in a secret interview, extorting a solemn oath of vengeance on the mother who had deprived him of his liberty and his empire. Broken in health and courage by close imprisonment, acting on a frame already yielding to the effects of unbridled indulgence, the young king was but a tool in the hands of Assarac, who soon conceived the idea of making him also a mere stepping-stone to the attainment of supreme power at which he aimed.

Though scrupulous in practising the usual forms and observances towards his lord, the eunuch scarcely affected to ignore his own real superiority, affirming only that his words and deeds were prompted by the immediate inspiration of his god.

'And Baal bids him store up goodly treasures for himself, you may be sure,' observed Kalmim, discussing with her old admirer the character of their new and arbitrary ruler; 'so that at any time he may win over the spearmen with spoil, as he secured the priests by promises, and the prophets of the grove by threats. Gold and steel, Sethos—these are the only real forces on earth, and I sometimes think there is no power that can dominate them in heaven.'

'Good faith,' answered Sethos, 'is precious as the one and true as the other. I have never wavered, Kalmim, in my loyalty to Ninyas, nor my love for *you*.'

'And what have they profited you?' she retorted lightly. 'You stood by the prince in good and evil, eating with him the bitter morsel and sharing the cup of affliction. One fine morning, Baal forsooth sends a fat man in white to pull the king of nations out of a prison-house and put him in a palace with a royal mantle on his shoulders, and a golden sceptre in his hand. Then comes the cup-bearer who has proved his readiness to go to the gates of death with his lord, and asks to be made leader of the host and to stand on the king's right hand, in the day of his glory as in the night of his bondage. What said Ninyas to the poor youth, in answer to so modest a request?'

'He laughed in my face,' replied the other, with considerable irritation. 'And if there is justice in heaven it will be repaid him fourfold. May the king live for ever!'

'So much for loyalty to a prince!' she continued. 'Now for truth to a woman. Have you *really* kept faith with me, Sethos, all this time? It is many a long day since you and I first met by a strange chance in the queen's paradise, and you told me—I forget what you told me, but it was something very foolish, no doubt.'

'You know I have,' said Sethos bitterly, almost fiercely, turning his head away while he spoke.

It was a short answer, but to a woman's ear worth a whole series of protestations. In perception of such matters, Kalmim was no whit behind her sex.

If he had but looked at her, he would have seen her blush, and surely in no encounter whatsoever should a man take his eye off his enemy. Sethos, alas, was completely at the adversary's mercy, and she trampled him accordingly.

'Well, and what has this service, also, profited you for your pains?' she asked in taunting accents, wholly unable to forbear the pleasure of tormenting him. 'You have stood by *me* at my need faithfully, nobly, grudging nothing, keeping nothing back. When the time comes, you will ask *me* too to make you my captain and leader, to seat you on my right hand till I die, and, Sethos, I too—I shall laugh in your face!'

'Be it so,' he answered in a grave quiet voice, so unlike his usual tones that she glanced anxiously towards him. He seemed sad and troubled, yet looked like a man whose loyalty was still unshaken and unimpeachable.

'And you are tired of it at last?' she asked, in the same mocking accents.

'It is too late to change now,' was his answer, with a wan and weary smile.

'Ninyas refused you?' she continued, looking straight into his eyes.

He bowed his head in silence.

'But *I* have only laughed at you,' she murmured, drawing her veil hastily over her face. 'And, Sethos, have you passed your life in Babylon and not found out that liking grows with laughter as blossoms come with rain? *I* am not a king, I am only a woman; and I cannot deny a faithful servant who asks the reward he has toiled through storm and sunshine to attain.'

He would have passed his arm round her waist, but with a dexterous twirl, the result, perhaps, of considerable practice, she placed herself out of reach.

'No,' she said with imposing force and gesture, 'my friend, and more than friend, this is not a time for follies such as these. Some day, when the heavy hand of Baal has been taken off this unhappy city, when men's flocks and herds and wives and children have ceased to be at the command of those who are but hewers of wood and drawers of water in the temple, I may peradventure suffer you to—to—well, to touch the tip of my finger with your lips. But now, the first duty of every son of Ashur is to cast off this hateful yoke that bows his nation to the dust. O that the old lion had but lived to see the white robes lording it in his well-beloved city! He would have cleared them out with fire and sword, ay, though all the host of heaven had come down from the stars to take their part.

'Look at *me!* O, I know well you never take your eyes off me if you can help it; but I am serious now. Look at *me*, I say—a woman who in her life before never knew a thought nor care weightier than the smoothing of a plait, the planting of a bodkin; I tell you I would take up spear and shield to-morrow, if I might help to lay Assarac and his priests in their blood at the altar before which they serve. What have they done for us? What has Baal himself done for us since he has governed from the throne of Nimrod? Corn is dear, water scarce, the people starve, and the priests wax fatter, prouder, fiercer, day by day. Even Beladon, who used to be meek and gentle as a weaned child, and was indeed a personable youth, and one of my truest friends—even Beladon, I say, holds that we are to be at his beck and call without question or murmur, you and I, and every one within the hundred gates of the city wall.'

'May Nisroch tear him limb from limb!' exclaimed Sethos, in high wrath; for he had long been jealous of the comely young priest's intimacy with Kalmim, and it was in no ignorance of his feelings that the latter now worked upon her listener with the hated name.

'Yes, Beladon,' she continued, 'though he be not so bad as some of the rest. But how long are we to bear this? How long are we to be trodden on and kept down, not by a conqueror of worlds like old Ninus, wielding bow and spear as I would handle a needle, but by a slothful priest, a eunuch forsooth, in flowing robes and linen tiara, who never lifted weapon deadlier than gilded fir-cone or fresh-gathered lotus, never bore heavier burden than jewelled casket, nor faced a fiercer enemy than the poor sheep he slays to please his god!'

'Nay, there you wrong him,' argued honest Sethos. 'If all that comes out of Armenia be true, never bolder champion mounted war-chariot than Assarac, the priest of Baal.'

'Armenia!' retorted Kalmim, with infinite contempt — 'a desert peopled by a few half-starved wretches, doubtless naked and without arms. Besides, was he not warring in the mountains under the banner of the Great Queen? I pray you, when did Semiramis ever fail to conquer where she set the battle in array? And now, by his own confession, she languishes with a death-wound, and he is not ashamed to be standing here within the brazen gates in a whole skin! O, it passes all patience! But I know my mistress well. Surely never yet was that shaft feathered which could drink her life-blood. Once I loved her dearly, and she repaid my faithful service with the gratitude of—of a Great Queen, I suppose! But for all that is past and gone, I will never believe, wounded or unwounded, she could abandon the sceptre of Nimrod, or license Baal himself to usurp her authority in the land of Shinar and the city she loves to call her own.'

'But Ninyas sits in the royal palace,' observed Sethos, 'under the mystic circle and the wings of gold. It is before Ninyas that the spearmen defile at noon, and to Ninyas that the people cry for justice in the gate at sunrise, when he is sober enough to hear.'

'And how often is that?' exclaimed Kalmim. 'Not once in twenty days. But are you too blind to perceive, O simple youth, that while Ninyas wears the tiara, Assarac holds the sceptre; while Ninyas fits the arrow, Assarac draws the bow? It is time Babylon were rid of both. The fire that crowns that sacred tower burns doubtless night and day; but what is that to me if it be so high up I cannot thread my needle in its light? When Baal means to rule over us in person, let him come down and show himself. I am tired of a god who never answers, call on him loudly as you will.'

Such liberal sentiments would have astonished her companion more, but that Sethos, during his lord's captivity, had dwelt long enough within its sacred precincts to have lost much of his former reverence for the mysteries of the temple, of his early confidence in the unseen power of its god. He felt somewhat bewildered, nevertheless, and astray in this uprooting of a faith that seemed like a birthright to every son of Ashur, and asked helplessly,

'If Baal cannot, and Ninyas must not, and Assarac will not, succour us, to whom then are we to look?'

'To the Great Queen,' answered Kalmim proudly: 'never believe but she will come again in her majesty, beautiful as morning, fierce and terrible as the storm that rises with mid-day. I have seen her angered once, only once in all my life. I tell you, Sethos, I would rather stand in the presence of Nisroch to be consumed than face the blaze of those eyes again. She spoke not, scarcely moved a limb; but I felt as the lamb must feel when the leopard has made her spring, and there is no escape. In her love, her hatred, and her desire, she knows no bounds and acknowledges no check, yet never sunlight was welcomed by captive in a dungeon as would be that beautiful face to-day in Babylon by the people of the Great Queen.'

While she spoke, she looked wistfully out over the desert towards the north; Sethos, watching her eager face, saw it brighten with a sudden gleam of triumph and hope. Following the direction of her eyes, he observed the flash of spears through a dense cloud low on the horizon, that denoted a body of horsemen on the march.

Pointing towards it, Kalmim burst into tears.

'It is the Great Queen!' she sobbed. 'For my sake, Sethos—for my sake, will you not be on our side?'

CHAPTER XVII.

BETRAYED.

PACING to and fro in the familiar cedar gallery, vexed, troubled, and impatient, Assarac shot glances of anger and defiance at the four-winged image of Nisroch, as though reproaching the god in whom he did *not* believe for withholding aid he would have considered it childish folly to implore. Though he had dispatched a messenger in eager haste to seek out the tents of the Anakim, and renew the offer of promotion he made to Sarchedon, so preoccupied was he, that Beladon had already prostrated himself more than once, ere his superior seemed conscious of his presence. The younger priest wondered to see the resolute and subtle eunuch so changed, so worn, so saddened. He marked the restless step, the sullen gesture, the moody unquiet eye, remembering, not without pity, a caged wild beast that had been trapped and brought into Babylon, long ago by certain hunters of the mountain, as a gift to the Great Queen.

Though a faithful servant enough, while a keener intellect and firmer spirit held him in subjection, he bethought him somewhat remorsefully it was time to leave his master now.

Assarac's eyes wandered over the other's figure with the unconscious stare of a sleep-walker ere they lightened into recognition, then he started and exclaimed, 'How now, Beladon? Returned so soon? What tidings of Semiramis?—I mean of Sarchedon, and the children of Anak with whom he dwells?'

'Let not my lord be wroth,' was the answer. 'Though his servant fled through the waste like an ostrich, yet was he wiser than that foolish bird, which plies her long legs and helpless wings to meet the storm of thunder and lightning she dreads. I have heard the thunder of the queen's chariots; I have seen the lightning of her spears. Instead of scouring the desert to seek the Anakim, lo, I turned bridle, and hastened back that I might warn my lord of her approach.'

Though something seemed to tell him the information was tantamount to a death-warrant, his heart leaped up with a wild unreasoning joy.

'The queen!' he exclaimed, while the blood flew to his wan heavy cheek. 'Is she then so near?'

'She will encamp to-night beneath the city walls,' answered Beladon imperturbably. 'She marches with the vanguard of her army; but the conquerors of Armenia cannot be many furlongs in her rear; and when the sun goes down to-morrow, the hosts of Ninyas will be increased fourfold, while the Great Queen lays her trophies and her sceptre at the feet of her son. May the king live for ever!'

Something in the cold sneering tones seemed to recall the eunuch's energies and wake him, as it were, from a dream.

'Never!' he muttered between his teeth; and seizing the other's arm in a gripe that caused him to wince with pain, he hurried out of the corridor, past the golden image of Baal, across the court of the temple, and so, through leafy thicket and level lawn, threaded its cool green paradise to the palace of the Great King.

Here Beladon, notwithstanding a sufficiently good opinion of his own merits, would have excused himself from entering; but Assarac's grasp was never relaxed, and ere the younger priest could realise the imprudence of such an intrusion, he found himself in the presence of one for whom he had been alternately spy and gaoler, yet who held over him irresponsible power of life and death.

Ninyas was seated in the shade on a chair of state, ornamented and embossed with the symbols of Assyrian sovereignty, under a trellis-work whereon had been trained the luxuriant tendrils of a vine, already bending and blushing in clusters of ripening grapes. A fountain scattered its silver spray in the sunshine, while female forms, with jetty locks, transparent veils, and glancing eyes, flitted through the shade. Soft airs murmured among the flowers, birds carolled from the thicket, and the king held a half-emptied goblet in his hand. With a hasty inclination of head and body, far short of the usual ceremony observed on entering the royal presence, Assarac placed himself in front of his lord, and looking him full in the face, arrested the cup that Ninyas was raising to his lips.

'Is this a time,' said he, in grave sonorous accents, 'for bubble of wine and sound of timbrel— for dance and song and careless revel—the mirth that goes before destruction—the folly that is a sure fore-runner of death? Rouse you, my lord, rouse you! Take bow in hand, gird your sword upon your thigh; for the watchman cries out on the wall, and even now your enemy is at the gate!'

The king's eyes, once so bright, looked dim and dull, the handsome features were flushed and soddened with excess; but he set his goblet down untasted, while there seemed something of interest, even apprehension, in the tone with which he asked, 'What enemy, and whence? I have but one in all the kingdoms of the earth, and she is sick unto death beyond the mountains of the north.'

Again, while he smiled in scorn, came a glow of triumph on the eunuch's weary face. 'Semiramis,' he answered, 'is encamped within bow-shot of the wall—Semiramis, the mother of my lord the king—Semiramis, who never cast a bank against a city but she razed it to the ground—who never drew bow but she shot her arrow home—who never took account of an injury but she requited it with death! O my queen, my queen!' he added in a broken murmur, 'even now the lord of earth trembles and cowers at the very whisper of your name!'

Ninyas turned pale. 'Counsel me, Assarac!' he exclaimed, while his eye roved helplessly over all the splendour and luxury that surrounded him. 'If my mother enters the city, I am undone.'

'Not so,' answered the eunuch. 'Let my lord the king go out to meet her as a son should welcome the mother of his affections bringing home the wife of his desire. Let the gates be thrown open, and the people give her greeting as she passes by. The hosts of the Great Queen are yet many a league off in the desert. Her vanguard, few in number, must be wearied sore with travel. When she enters her own city, who so fitting to provide for her safety as the son of her vows? Let him guard her like the apple of his eye, and relieve her of all care in the government of the people whom he rules.'

'You know her not!' exclaimed Ninyas, much disturbed. 'Where is the prison-house in Babylon that could hold her for a single day? Where is the son of Ashur who would not leap to the saddle with bow and spear at the first wave of the Great Queen's hand?'

The eunuch's answer came in firm and measured accents, though his face was distorted as with a hidden agony of pain.

'There is a prison-house from which not Ashtaroth herself could break out—from which old Nimrod might not be delivered by all the horsemen of Assyria.

When my lord's servants shall surround and hew her in pieces, then may every son of Ashur bind on his headpiece a shred of the Great Queen's garments, whom he loved so well.'

Ninyas laughed aloud, and, seizing his discarded goblet, drained it to the dregs.

'Enough!' he exclaimed. 'She sinned against Nisroch and Baal, when she took the sceptre of Nimrod from the hand of his descendant. What am I, that I should interfere to avert her doom? And yet, I would it might be done without shedding of blood. Can we not lead her forth from the city into some desert place, and so dispose of her in safety, where she shall disturb the king no more?'

'Will my lord trust his servant?' asked the eunuch.

'I will remain here at the banquet in my palace until it is over,' answered Ninyas brutally. 'Let Baal be his own avenger, and let Assarac see to vindicating the honour of his god. I have spoken.' Then, clapping his hands, Ninyas summoned back the women who usually surrounded him at his revels, to dismiss the whole matter from his mind in a deep and stupefying carouse.

Leaving the royal presence, Beladon felt his

arm seized once more in the eunuch's painful gripe, while Assarac muttered, half-unconsciously, such broken sentences as served to disclose the plot he had constructed, and the means by which it was to be carried out. Presently, in a few simple directions, he imparted to his subordinate the outline of his purpose, commanding him to muster all the priests and prophets in the city at the great northern gate by which the queen should enter, with knife and lotus-flower in hand; to surround these with so strong a force of spearmen as it would be impossible for the populace to break through; and then, at a given signal, to fall on Semiramis with his followers, bind her in fetters of iron, and so bring her a helpless captive into the temple of Baal. It would be a fine revenge, thought Assarac, to keep her there till the arrival of Sarchedon from the desert, and then to slay them, in each other's sight, before the altar of his god. Better still, perhaps, and worthier of his fierce mad love, to strike his own knife into her heart at the first halt of her chariot within the gate.

'I can trust you,' said he, when they parted, and Beladon proposed to attest his fidelity in a great oath by the everlasting wings, 'because the queen's first act, when she reënters the city, will be to take vengeance on him who kept the door of her son's prison-house, and suffered the captive to escape.'

But the wariest of mankind may leave one weak point undefended—the keenest judges of human nature will omit from their calculation some vice, prejudice, or folly, such as dominates the very self-interest of their tools. That Beladon should have disclosed a plot, on the success of which his own personal safety, his very life depended, would have been unaccountable, but for the joyous, pleasure-loving disposition which, priest of Baal though he was, could not keep his secret from a woman.

Kalmim had beguiled him out of every particular before sundown, affecting, the better to deceive him, an irreconcilable enmity to the Great Queen, and entire devotion in the service of her son.

If a woman makes up her mind to duplicity, a little more or a little less counts as nothing to her conscience. She finds it as easy to profess an affection she does not feel, and a candour of which she is incapable, as to push another bodkin into her hair, lay another coat of red or white on the cheek she is not ashamed to paint. When Kalmim had resolved she would take him into captivity, it was no more possible for Beladon to resist than for the bird to escape out of the snare of the fowler. And, although the latter was exceedingly lavish of smiles and liberal of promises, the prey found itself captured, plumed, and despoiled, with no material equivalent for utter discomfiture and disgrace.

More than a match for a score of priests, she could indeed have outwitted the whole male population of Babylon, but that she too had found her master, and was but a weak foolish woman in presence of the man she loved.

To him she betook herself in her distress, imploring him to interfere at such a juncture, and prevent a crime which, with all his loyalty to his prince, seemed to Sethos too foul and unnatural to contemplate.

'There is danger also for *you*,' she exclaimed, wringing her hands, and sobbing in real perplexity. 'No son of Ashur must leave the city to-night on pain of death; and yet, if the queen be not forewarned, nothing can save her from the vengeance of these blood-thirsty priests. O Sethos, Sethos, did I not love you dearly, I had never trusted you with such a mission; yet how can I bear to send you out into the very jaws of death?'

But the cup-bearer's equanimity was proof even against so formidable a consideration. Accepting her confession of attachment with a good-humoured carelessness that at any other time would have cut her to the quick, he professed his readiness to incur any amount of peril, so that he might preserve Semiramis from the threatened assault, and her son from the commission of so hideous an outrage. It was agreed, therefore, that he should escape from the city at all hazards, and make his way to the tent of the Great Queen, under cover of night. To leave Babylon through any one of her gates was impracticable, so closely were they guarded by the spearmen of Ninyas under Assarac's orders; and it was only by watching a favourable opportunity during the darkest hours before the moon had risen, that Kalmim succeeded in letting her lover down from the wall by a rope, to dispatch him on his errand of life and death.

With characteristic coolness the cup-bearer received his instructions and embarked on his perilous enterprise; but Kalmim, though not a nerve failed her while, swinging in mid-air, his life depended on her steadiness of hand, had over-taxed her strength; for no sooner was the tension of the rope relaxed, and the form of Sethos lost in darkness as he sped from beneath the wall, than brain and sense gave way, leaving her pale, prostrate, and helpless on the ground.

CHAPTER XVIII.

WHO IS ON MY SIDE?

RECONCILED to their change of rulers under the crafty administration of Assarac, careless who swayed the sceptre of Nimrod so long as wine was cheap and corn plentiful, the people of Babylon troubled themselves but little that the Armenian expedition seemed so tardy in returning; that Semiramis lay sick and dying, as they were told, among those northern mountains; or that Ninyas, whom they had been taught to believe a dutiful son abdicating in his mother's favour, reigned once more in her stead. Nevertheless, even among that fierce and fickle populace remained a leaven of the adoration she alone was able to inspire, and every child of Ashur at home or a-field felt his dignity, his self-love, and his nationality identified with the glory of the Great Queen.

They were stirred more than the eunuch expected

by the news of her return; so that when it became known she was within bow-shot of the wall, and about to reënter her own especial city, Assarac's watchful eye discerned among the multitude those signs of discontent and restlessness which precede a tumult, as lowering clouds and whitened waves indicate the coming of a storm.

Groups were forming and dispersing in the street, women and children remained on the roofs and terraces of their houses, men looked expectant in each other's faces; while captains and warriors thronged the ramparts, as though an enemy were already at the gate.

Presently there came a hush and calm over all that vast assemblage, succeeded by a shiver that stirred the rippling mass from edge to edge, when the tramp of horses, the roll of a chariot, broke on the still warm air; then, wild and fierce as a defiance, though loud, jubilant, and overwhelming, rose a mighty shout from great Babylon to welcome back her queen.

Assarac, eager and preoccupied, watching these signs of earth with more anxiety than he had ever read the stars, felt a momentary thrill of triumph in that very enthusiasm which, uncontrolled by his own skill, must herald his doom. For a moment, in the agony of conflicting feelings, he thought it would be well could he abandon every scheme of glory and greatness, forego pride, ambition, revenge, to die at the queen's feet, and be at rest. Gazing on her as she drew near in the chariot, this temporary weakness passed away, leaving all that was evil in his nature to resume the ascendency once more. Could this be the proud Semiramis, the bright, the matchless, the beautiful? this sad and stately woman, pale with the long fatigue of woe, yet wearing in her desolation the same unrivalled beauty that had enhanced the glory of her pride? It seemed the ghost of her former self, thus bending its haughty head in acknowledgment of a nation's greeting, as she passed within the gate—a spirit too sad to be of good, too fair to be of evil, sublimed and elevated by the prescience of its doom, catching and reflecting the spectral rays of a cold clear light that dawns beyond the grave.

Had she glowed, as was her wont, in all the flush and sparkle of her imperial charms, he could have found it in his heart to have spared her even then; for her dear sake, could have betrayed his followers, broken faith with his king, and forsworn himself before his god. But marking the sorrow she did not care to hide, and remembering its cause, his blood turned to gall, and he vowed with bitter oaths she should never light down from that chariot a living woman—no, not if he must hew her in pieces with his own hand.

But for the Great Queen to be forewarned was to be forearmed. In no extremity of sorrow nor of danger was it possible for her to lose that unconscious presence of mind, that instinctive power of combination, which had made her the conqueror of the world. Informed by Sethos of the conspiracy against her life, she had taken measures to defeat it wisely, calmly, promptly, yet deliberately, just as she would have sat down to besiege a fenced city, or gone out to meet an enemy in the open field. While the eunuch waited to hem her in with his priests and spearmen, Semiramis, watching her opportunity, foiled him by the suddenness of her attack.

Halting her chariot in the open space immediately within the gate, and taking advantage of the astonished silence which succeeded this unexpected stoppage, the Great Queen stood erect, flung her arms above her head, and cried with a loud voice, 'Who is on my side?' Then Assarac knew that, by so much time as it took to speak those words, he was too late; and immediately before his eyes there passed a darkness, that was as the shadow of death.

From her people, who loved the very ground she trod on, rose an outcry to which their previous shouts had been but a maiden's whisper compared to the roar of a beast of prey. Swords leaped from the scabbard, strong arms beat the air, dark eyes gleamed, and dark-curled beards bristled with fierce enthusiasm, eager hate, or wild desire for blood— archers and spearmen descended like a torrent from the wall, stout champions of a hundred battles came rushing and crowding through the streets. They gathered in swarms about their queen; they hemmed her in with a circle of steel; they swore, they wept, they gnashed their teeth, they implored, they adjured her only to point out an enemy, and they would tear him limb from limb.

Never before, through all the years she reigned in Babylon, had her power seemed so absolute, her dominion so secure; yet she knew, none better, that had her outcry been deferred by one short minute, had she halted her chariot but fifty paces farther on within the city, a score of blades would have carved away life and sorrow together from her aching heart, her cheek, now so cold and pale in its bereavement, would have been for ever cold and pale in death.

But not a shade of colour deepened that lovely cheek; no glitter of wrath, nor anxiety, nor even excitement of mortal strife, disturbed the scorn of those calm proud eyes, while she pointed to the eunuch, standing erect in his chariot over against her, and spoke in the clear full tones that had so often turned the tide of battle, like the trumpets of a succouring host.

'I have need of that man!' said she, stretching out her round white arm. 'Sons of Ashur, I bid you fall on Assarac, priest of Baal. Slay him not, but bind him and bring him to me!'

He was no coward, yet he trembled in every joint. Perhaps the sound of her voice moved him no less than the yells of rage, the scowls of hatred, the flashes of steel that met him on every side, than the mighty rush that made at him, wave on wave, as the wolves of the forest pour on some wounded mountain bull to get him down.

He bore himself bravely, notwithstanding, calling priests and spearmen to his rescue, fitting an arrow to the bow he was never to draw again. For a moment his white-clad form towered above the press and tumult, like a sail in a troubled sea, that disappears among the breakers ere a man has summoned courage for a second look. The priests of Baal could not resist the shock. In spite of numbers and discipline, the hired spearmen gave way. There was a rush, a recoil, an angry roar, a scuffle of feet, the crash of a broken chariot, the scream of a woman from the house-tops, a horse reared high above their heads, the surging crowd divided, and on the open space emerged some half a score Assyrian warriors, dragging in their midst Assarac, priest of Baal, to the feet of the Great Queen.

Even now in this extremity of danger and disgrace, bruised, panting, dishevelled, doomed to certain death, he sought in the queen's eyes for something of sympathy, of recognition, of acknowledgment, that they had once looked kindly in his own. Of all he suffered, this was perhaps the keenest pang—that on the fair face he had loved, and hated, and worshipped so madly, there showed no more of anger than of pity. Immovable, impenetrable, but for her beauty she might have been an image of Nisroch the avenger, god of retribution and of fate.

Then he laughed out loud, a strange harsh laugh that scared the guards who held him, while he thought that here in his mortal anguish, throbbing under the knife or writhing on the stake, he had power to wring and torture that proud heart still.

Before deigning to notice him, she thanked her people for their loyalty with a sad and weary smile.

'Sons of Ashur,' said she, 'let none persuade you I have ever believed you could fail your queen. She has but trusted you once more to-day, and nobly have you once more answered her appeal. I have spoiled for you another city; I have conquered for you another kingdom; I have journeyed far and fast to return to you. My bow is unstrung, my sword is sheathed, and I would fain rest from my labours. But Ashtaroth sleeps not in heaven, nor Semiramis on earth; and be the queen's eyes never so heavy, justice must be done by the greatest, as by the least, through the length and breadth of the land of Shinar. There is one here who has imagined evil in his heart against his ruler. Assarac, priest of Baal, what have you to say why you should not forthwith be put to death?'

With these last syllables she turned full upon him her deep inscrutable eyes, and if he had any hope of it before, he neither desired nor expected pardon now. The pitiless gaze chilled him to the marrow, while he felt, that were their positions reversed, he too could be as cold and calm and cruel as his judge.

One glance of sympathy in the crowd would have unmanned him; but he looked for it in vain. On earth he saw a dreary wavering mass of sullen faces, and in heaven a wide-winged vulture, wheeling, hovering, poising itself in the blue eternal sky.

It was not his god that sustained him now, nor his sacred character, nor his priestly lore; not even the stubborn pride engrained in the nature of such spirits, destined to affect the fate of dynasties and trouble the security of an empire. No; he took refuge in the bitterness of that despair which has found and proved the worst—when love turns to hate, and faith to scorn—when the sweet springs of hope are poisoned at their source, and the vision of an angel in a halo of light changes to a mocking fiend, or a bare gaunt skeleton crowned with a grinning skull.

He returned a stare of defiance, calm and comtemptuous as her own.

'It is for the Great Queen to reward her servants according to their deserts,' said he. 'Let her ask herself if I have merited death at her hands.'

'It is not Semiramis who accuses you,' she retorted coldly. 'By the laws of Shinar you are judged, and by them you are condemned. I have spoken.'

There was no hope; none. Yet would she but look kindly on him, he could bear it bravely, he thought, and die in his utter weariness, as a man lies down to sleep. He made one last effort.

'Have I not served her,' he asked, 'through good and evil, in no hope of payment or reward, but for the love and loyalty I bore to the Great Queen? I have lived too long when the face of Semiramis is turned from me in anger. I ask for no pardon, no reprieve. Let her but say that she forgives me before I die!'

'I have nothing to forgive,' she replied, with pitiless unconcern. 'The servant has raised his hand against his ruler; the subject has conspired against his queen. Whose are these white-robed bands cowering and trembling before me, though each man carries a naked knife in his girdle, and another in his hand? Who drew up that sullen and dejected line of warriors, instructing them to bend their bows and point their spears against the leader they have followed to victory? It is not for Semiramis to ask the question, but Assyria. It is not for Semiramis to answer it, but Baal, and he cries with a loud voice, "Assarac the priest!"'

'Who turned on her at the last!' he shouted, in a paroxysm of fury and despair. 'Who bears here in his bosom the secret she would give all her empire to obtain; but who defies and reviles the Great Queen to her face, even in the jaws of death!'

She started, and for a moment seemed uncertain how to act; but recovering herself, pronounced firmly the fatal words, 'Cover his face, and lead him forth. I have spoken.'

It was a sentence that could never be annulled. The eunuch felt he was doomed, and glanced instinctively upward, where the vulture passed between him and the sun.

So they brought the hideous stake, and impaled him in sight of all men, that the people of Babylon might pass by to rebuke him with scoffs and curses, for a traitor who had lifted his hand against the Great Queen.

Two days, two nights, he writhed and languished in his agony. On the third morning men had become wearied of him, and he was left alone, save that the vulture floating overhead kept watch on untiring wing, and waited for him still.

At sunrise there came a veiled woman, with a jar of water in her hand. His dim eye lightened, and the spasm, that should have been a smile, crossed his face, for he recognised in her gait and bearing the presence of his queen.

She raised her veil to look fixedly on those dying features, so changed, so distorted — to mark the quiver of those dry cracked lips, the flutter of life that played over the blackened, withered frame.

'Speak,' said she, in a low hoarse whisper, while the water rippled pleasantly in its jar. 'Speak, and I will have mercy; for you shall drink and die.'

He nodded assent, eying with piteous eagerness the deadly draught for which he longed.

'Doth he live?' she asked, and laid the jar almost against his lips.

Another nod, a convulsive choking gasp, and a roll of the half-closed eyes.

'And where?' she continued, in fierce impatience, pitiless of his sufferings, careless of all but the secret she was fain to extort, even from the dead.

It was obvious that till his lips were moistened he could not answer, if he would. She held the jar to his mouth, and he took such a long and greedy draught as dulled his mortal agony with a sense of relief from suffering that was almost joy.

Again she watched those baked black lips with jealous eyes. They strove to form a word that yet died on them ere it could be uttered. Was it in mockery they trembled with certain faint syllables, that to her sense of sight, rather than hearing, seemed to indicate the desert? Was it in mockery they smiled and writhed and gibbered ere they set themselves, fixed and rigid for evermore?

Semiramis turned thoughtfully away, and the vulture came swooping down; for he, too, had waited long and patiently to take his share of one who had been a reader of the stars, a governor of the empire, the Great Queen's favourite servant, Assarac, high-priest of Baal.

CHAPTER XIX.

FORGIVEN.

For two days, woe, perplexity, and dire confusion reigned in the temple of the great Assyrian god. Baal might be an hungered, but they slew for him no droves of sheep and oxen; athirst, but they poured him out no drink-offerings; displeased, but they sought not favour and forgiveness with praise and prayer, because his servants looked in vain for a high-priest to interpret the commands of their deity, and the great golden image, towering sullen, and unmoved, afforded neither word nor sign. The denizens of the temple stared blankly in each other's faces, for men doubted sore in this crisis of the Assyrian hierarchy whose turn it might next be to die.

But on the third day, court and temple were once more redolent of incense and bright with flowers;

altars blazed, victims fell, ditches ran crimson with blood. A hundred priests leaped, howled, and cut themselves with knives, a thousand voices raised their hymn of triumph, and Beladon, chosen by direct interposition of his god, under the authority of Ninyas his king, was proclaimed high-priest of Baal, in place of the dead man, crouched yonder on his stake in an open space near the northern gate, already torn and mangled out of human likeness by the birds of prey.

Careless of a fallen master, the new high-priest had turned gladly from Assarac to obtain favour in the sight of Ninyas; and that prince was content to give him honour and promotion in the mean time, waiting his own leisure to destroy him without pity or remorse.

For on this third day, the son of Ninus again sat in the gate to administer justice, again shook off the fetters of sloth, and the drowsiness of wine-cups, to wear the royal tiara of his fathers, and carry the sceptre of Nimrod in his hand.

The people of Babylon indeed clamoured loudly for their queen, crowding the streets and terraces about her palace, rending the air with their cries, vowing vengeance on priest and prophet, if she forbore to show herself, and even threatening the sacred person of her son.

It needed all the influence of a priesthood bribed by gifts and promises, all the intimidation of an army corrupted by gold and spoil, to persuade them that she had left her faithful subjects for the realm of those divinities to whom she was akin, and that the white doves they had seen since sunrise, flitting on restless pinions through her favourite city, were but so many messengers from the spirit-world, bidding a nation of mourners take comfort for the departure of the Great Queen.

It was to Beladon that Ninyas intrusted the promulgation of this strange belief, resolving that so soon as the tumult had subsided, so soon as he was himself firmly established on the throne, it would be wise to destroy the only power that rivalled his own in the land of Shinar, by the slaughter of their new high-priest, and general destruction of the worship of Baal, in favour of Nebo, Nisroch, or some other deity, over whose servants he would take care to retain undisputed influence and control.

For in the golden morning, lying tossing and troubled on his couch, a deep sleep had fallen on Ninyas, even with the rising of the sun, and he had dreamed a dream, or seen a vision, such as moved even that heart of his, so hardened by years of vice and self-indulgence, brought the unaccustomed tears to those eyes blinded by folly, sensuality, and sin.

He dreamed that he was a child once more—a tender happy child, triumphant in a new toy, or a treasure of fruit and flowers, loving, hopeful, and believing in his mother, the queen, as he believed in the light of day. He thought she came to his bedside carrying a fair and bending lotus in her hand; that she withheld from him the flower, resisting alike his prayers, his caresses, and his tears; that in his impatience and childish wrath, he seized the white caressing hand and bit it till the blood came, striking and buffeting the while so fiercely that his efforts seemed to wake him, and yet he could not rise, though he knew that he lay there a grown man, stretched on his own royal couch, struggling with the influence of a dream.

He must be helpless, he felt, and passive—chilled, shivering, speechless—so long as those reproachful eyes held him in their gaze, so long as that stately figure bent over him so tenderly, that pale sad face confronted his own in the shadow of an unearthly beauty, that awed him with the majesty of death.

His tongue clave to the roof of his mouth, yet it seemed loosened, and his senses were freed from their heaviest restraint, when the vision addressed him; for was it not his mother's voice? And in spite of the injuries she had inflicted, in spite of injustice, treachery, all that had come and gone, those tones were liquid with a music that could still dominate his spirit, still soften and subdue his heart. 'Ninyas,' she said, 'beloved, has it come to this, that my son could thirst for his mother's blood?' He almost believed while she spoke there were red drops on the white hand that had tended and fondled him from a child. Twice he raised his eyes to hers, and cast them down in very shame; twice he essayed an answer, and his lips refused to form the words; but the third time he took courage, and, with a great effort, exclaimed, 'Forgive me, mother; for I have sinned! I am unworthy to reign in Shinar; I am unworthy even to draw bow among the sons of Ashur! Yet forgive me, mother; for am I not your son?'

A smile, unspeakably sad and tender, came over the pale fair face. 'I have forgiven,' said she, 'although the arrow from my son's quiver bit into my very heart. Listen, Ninyas: it was foretold long ago, by one who read the stars, and who knows doubtless, ere now, whether he read them right—it was foretold, I say, by this wise man, that when the spear on which she leaned at her utmost need should break and wound her hand, then must the doves that nourished her childhood come back to lead Semiramis away, and the sons of Ashur must wander to and fro through old Nineveh and mighty Babylon, and all the wide bounds of the land of Shinar, asking each other in vain for tidings of the Great Queen. I mourned in sorrow and sadness, but my son was yet left to me, and I leaned on him as his father was wont to lean after battle on his spear. My spear is broken, my son has failed me; he would reign unvexed, unwearied by the counsels of his mother. Go to! He will never look on that mother's face again.'

He fell into a great sweat and trembling; with a desperate effort, he leaped like a young lion from his couch, to fall at her feet and clasp her knees, and detain her even by force, that he might make amends. Alas, he grasped the empty air! He searched in vain with eager gaze throughout the chamber, and looked only on coloured carvings and vermilion roof, on alabaster columns, scarlet hangings, winged monsters tipped with gold, all the pomp and symbols of imperial sovereignty, his own without question now, because she was gone for evermore. Then he burst into a passion of tears, and so, draining the flagon of Damascus wine that stood by his couch, felt comforted, and went out among his people with diadem and sceptre, feeling in his heart, that at last he was really an Assyrian king.

As the day waned, and the populace, who had been feasted at the royal expense, found themselves refreshed with food and gladdened by wine, discontent gave way to hilarity, and anxiety for the fate of their queen lapsed into easy indifference, or a stupid satisfaction in those supernatural attributes, by which they were taught to account for her disappearance.

It was credited of all men that she had been claimed by the unearthly order of beings to which she belonged; that she had only been intrusted for a time to the Assyrians, for the completion of their national glory; and that now, having fulfilled her mission, she was summoned back by kindred spirits, who, in the form of doves, birds she always prized and cherished, were to-day flitting in unusual numbers about the city of her choice.

Kalmim, whose eyes were red with weeping,

stoutly supported the general belief, finding in it, no doubt, a salve for certain qualms of conscience she could not but entertain, regarding her own varying loyalty towards the mistress she served. This nimble-tongued tirewoman found herself regretting many a hint she had thrown out, many a petty scandal she had promulgated in derision of the Great Queen. To have seen her back in the royal palace, to have smoothed her robes, tired her head, and done her bidding once more, Kalmim would willingly have given all she prized in the world, except perhaps the affection of Sethos, whom she now claimed as her own possession, by every rite of love and law known in the land of Shinar.

Standing with him on a house-top over against the temple of Baal, and marking with fond eyes how his bright young face glowed in the parting rays of a sun already touching the horizon of the desert, she could not forbear a sigh of pity for one whose lot, in spite of beauty, glory, and power, seemed so dark and sad, compared to her own.

'She had everything Baal and Ashtaroth could bestow,' observed Kalmim, looking lovingly in her companion's face. 'And see what has been the end. To hover, like an evil spirit, saddened and restless, about the place that is still bright with her glory, and then to vanish, none can tell where, like a cloud that comes up from the desert with promise of rain, and while man and beast are yet a-thirst to welcome it, lo, it has passed over, and is gone.'

'We shall see her no more,' answered Sethos. 'Nor shall we see one like unto her again. Since Ashur came down from the stars to lead them, his children have known but one Great Queen. Of a surety, it is enough! Another Ashtaroth would set the heavens in a blaze; another Semiramis would be too much for the vexed earth to sustain.'

She glanced at him sharply, but his features wore their usual expression of placid and somewhat languid content.

'She was not happy,' said Kalmim, as if puzzled to account for the anomaly. 'And yet she had wisdom, fame, courage, riches, unlimited empire, and, O Sethos, beauty surpassing even the daughters of the stars!'

'The last is the gift you grudge her most,' observed the cup-bearer, with a quiet smile, as of one who directs his shaft, though without malice, straight towards its mark.

But instead of flushed denial or indignant retort,

he was surprised to note on Kalmim's face an expression of real apprehension. She turned quite pale, while she replied,

'It is a fatal possession for the owner, when spoilers can be found who scruple not to share in it by the strong hand. O Sethos,' she added, with a shudder, pointing to the temple of Baal, 'there is but one man I fear in the whole of Babylon, and he stands, night and morning, before the altar of his god, the second in power through all the land of Shinar, after my lord the king.'

Sethos laughed outright, whereat, in Kalmim's eyes, displeasure took the place of fear.

'Listen,' said he, 'and remember that I am not given to vain words, but that I speak only so much as I surely know. Do you dread the handful of bleached bones, the few dangling strips of blackened flesh, that were once that famous eunuch who made himself chief counsellor of princes, mightiest leader of armies in all Assyria, and great interpreter of the god he worshipped, to rule, as it seemed, rather than to obey? I tell you, Kalmim, that Assarac, withering yonder on his stake, is as much to be feared as comely Beladon, now high-priest of Baal. I tell you that I had rather change places with the one who has known and proved the worst than with the other, who has yet to learn the mercies of Ninyas for such as thwart his projects or stand in the way of his convenience.'

'What mean you?' she asked. 'Are you in the secrets of my lord the king?'

'He has shown favour to his servant,' answered the other, with mock gravity, 'since the days of his youth, when I filled his cup to the brim at the bidding of Ninus, now driving a golden chariot amongst the stars. He has not forgotten that I waited dutifully at his footstool, while he wore sackcloth in his prison-house, as he had been clad in purple on a throne. Above all, he remembers that, but for me, he would have sinned a hideous sin against the Great Queen; therefore is my place at his right hand in his secret chamber; therefore can I tell you, Kalmim, that Beladon and his priests are doomed, and that the jackals you hear now howling beneath the wall shall scarcely wait another moon ere they tear them limb from limb. Beladon is thine enemy and mine. What am I that I should set myself against the counsels of my lord the king?'

She drew a deep sigh of relief. The tirewoman was happy now, and had reached the haven of her rest; yet, even in her fulness of content, there crept a dreary sadness about her heart, while she thought on the vanished glories of the mistress she had served and loved, marvelling, even while she mourned, at the strange departure and sad mysterious fate of the Great Queen.

CHAPTER XX.

LOST IN THE DARK.

As in the heart of man, seared, desolate, and lonely though it be, there remains a tender spot, bearing remembrance of the tears that freshened it long ago; so in the wildest tract of desert is hidden some green and pleasant place where, even should the leaf be faded or the well-spring dry, lingers a certain sense of peace, freshness, and repose, a faint but precious echo from the drip and murmur of the drowsy waters, and the breeze whispering through the palms.

In such a refuge, many a league from the stir and turmoil of crowded Babylon, had Sarchedon unstrung his bow, and laid his spear aside.

Notwithstanding the promises of Assarac, and the promptings of a martial spirit, he had yielded to the persuasions of her he loved, satisfied, after all his perils and adventures, to have gained the one treasure he coveted, and to keep it in his own possession for evermore.

Under the protection of his adopted brethren—for the Anakim, overlooking comparative deficiency of stature in consideration of courage and prowess, had received him into their tribe—and secured on all sides by the unbroken expanse of desert that surrounded him, he felt he had nothing to dread from the vengeance of Ninyas, nor even from pursuit by the Great Queen. These might rule unquestioned over many a fair and fertile province of their mighty empire, bearing absolute sway wherever forest waved or river flowed, wherever brick was laid on brick for human habitation, or smiling surface, tilled by human hands, grew fat with corn, and wine, and oil; but was not their boundless waste the heritage of the sons of Anak? and scouring it at all seasons, as in all directions, how were they to be eluded by assailants who would penetrate into their dominion? what tactics or what stratagems could foil those watchful eyes, keen as the vulture's poised in their burning sky, those matchless horses, swift and untiring as the wind that swept their desert sands?

'We are indeed safe, my beloved,' said Sarchedon, after recapitulating the many difficulties with which an enemy who sought them would have to contend. 'Safer here than we should be in the fortress of Ascalon, guarded by wall and rampart, bristling with bow and spear; for while the chariots of our foes were labouring far beyond the horizon, one of our long-limbed brethren would come galloping lightly in to give us warning, and even if they ever reached our nest, it would be cold many hours before they found it. I should be loth to leave it too,' he added, surveying with extreme content the pleasant refuge in which they had taken up their rest; 'for in all the paradises of Babylon was never so green and lovely a spot as this!'

Contrasted with the arid waste that stretched around them to the sky, it seemed, indeed, a fair and peaceful retreat. Like the mirage of the desert, it was adorned by a knot of waving palms, a glittering lake, a breadth of verdant pasture, a thicket of tufted grass, bending reeds, and aromatic shrubs. Like the mirage too, it was difficult to find, but unlike the mirage, it was dotted with a goats' hair tent, at the door of which, smiling and unveiled, she sat for whose sake Sarchedon had abandoned friends, fame, ambition, country: his treasure, his pearl of price, the fairest woman in all the earth—but one.

'I dread only Ninyas,' said Ishtar. 'For I know the young king's wilful spirit, and the proud heart that cannot endure to be crossed or thwarted in its desire. Only Ninyas for myself,' she added, with a wistful smile, 'and—and the Great Queen for you.'

'The Great Queen!' he repeated, laughing lightly. 'Ere now I must surely have had more than one successor, and doubtless I am forgotten, as though I had never been; indeed I hope—I hope it may be so.'

While he reiterated his wish, she looked sharply and inquiringly in his face, withdrawing her eyes, however, in some confusion, when his glance met her own. He perceived it not, and Ishtar scarce knew whether she was vexed or gratified to mark how the jealous anxieties of love had thus been quenched in the frank confidence of possession, but on reflection set his blindness down to the engrossing nature of his occupation, for he was busy shaping one of those short thick clubs used by desert horsemen in chase of the ostrich, to be hurled at the bird's long legs, while they rode her down.

'I shall be back at sunset,' said he, putting the finishing touch to his wooden weapon, and loosing the tether of his horse ere he sprang to the saddle, 'then shall Ishtar have at her tent-door such a tuft of plumes as were never seen even before the pavilion of the Great King.'

She was scanning the far horizon with anxious eyes. 'I pray you go not forth, beloved,' she murmured. 'There is a dull blurred line yonder, where sand and sky meet. Already the whirlwind is stirring in his sleep. Surely, he will wake up in his fury before night.'

Her lord laughed and shook his bridle, waving a light farewell as he rode away; while Ishtar turned wistfully into the tent and wondered if he never regretted enterprise, fame, ambition, all he had foregone for her sake; if he never let his thoughts wander back to the matchless beauty and fatal smile of the Great Queen.

So the woman pondered, half in sadness, asking untoward questions of her own anxious heart, and the man sped merrily over the plain, rejoicing in the freedom of the saddle, leaving care to plod hopelessly in his tracks, as he galloped on.

But though his eye brightened and his soul rejoiced, because of the boundless waste and the free desert air, there was death in his right hand. The poor ungainly ostrich lay bleeding at his feet, her legs broken by his skill, her wings despoiled of their precious tufts, to make a gift for the woman he loved.

The sun was yet high when he turned bridle towards his home, and peering about him in search of those scarce perceptible inequalities on its surface, which form the landmarks of the wilderness, he found cause to remember Ishtar's warning; while for a moment his heart stood still, with a sense of coming danger, such as braces the brave man for mortal conflict, and bids the coward tremble with mortal fear.

Where the palms that nodded above his tent should have broke the level sky-line, there was no horizon now. Only shifting misty shadows, dull, dim, and tawny, a fusion of earth and heaven. He could bear to look on the sun too, glowing yonder like a ball of burnished copper, and he knew what that rim of violet foretold—a cruel portent—beautiful exceedingly.

There was a falling glitter in the air, as if it were raining gold, and his horse snorted violently, betraying symptoms of restlessness and alarm. O for Merodach now! Merodach, whose bones were bleaching far away, where the dead lay in heaps under the wall of Ardesh.

He pressed into a gallop, nevertheless; for a dun

cloud-like column, growing in height and volume as it approached, was moving steadily towards him, in many whirls and gyrations, yet, fast as he rode, gaining on him with every stride. The sky had darkened, and the fine particles of sand with which the air was filled blistered his skin, choking his nostrils and penetrating into his very lungs.

Then the mighty rush of the whirlwind roared in his ears, turning his linen head-dress over his face, driving man and horse before it in an opaque impenetrable cloud of sand.

He had once dreamed of such a death. Could this be his fate, and had it indeed overtaken him at last?

He thought of Ishtar at the tent-door, looking for one who never came; he thought of the other woman who had loved him—his temptation, his evil spirit, his enemy, beautiful and wicked, Semiramis the Great Queen.

Driving on, as a ship at sea drives before the tempest, he was aware of certain phantom shapes, some few spear-lengths off, that loomed gigantic in the fatal cloud. Were they real or but creatures of his brain, already maddened by a sense of suffocation? Perhaps demons of the simoon, triumphant, derisive, rejoicing in his destruction. No; they were surely earthly forms—two or three horsemen plunging up to their girths, and a dromedary in the midst. Were they waving to him for help, or only struggling and gesticulating in blind perplexity, in the agony of a fierce despair? The whirlwind drove him nearer, nearer yet. He could distinguish the reddened eye of the dromedary, and its distended nostril craving for a breath of air, while choked with sand.

There came another mighty rush and roar to stun him as with a blow. Half conscious, he was aware of a face that moved before him through the gloom like a vision of the night—a dreamy face, calm, fearless, beautiful, smiling its sad farewell. Even at such extremity his heart leaped up with keen guilty throbs, for in that passing vision it recognised the face of the Great Queen.

Deeper and thicker grew the darkness; louder and fiercer roared the storm. A gleam of white seemed to flit before his eyes ere they were blinded by the driving sand. His horse struggled, fell, and rose again, trembling with exhaustion and fear; but the air had cleared now, and he could see, half a bow-shot before him, a fair dove winging her flight calmly on towards the light of day. Looking back to where his peril had been shared by those shadowy wayfarers, he only noticed a few slight undulations on the surface of the desert—a rolling wave or two of sand to mark the terrible track of the simoon, and hide his buried secrets, whatever they might be.

Following the dove, as it flitted before him, Sarchedon rode slowly on, pondering many things in his heart, but never taking his eyes off the bird that was guiding him home. At sunset, lighting down beneath the palms he loved, it circled twice round his head and disappeared within the darkness of his tent.

Entering in, he was encircled by the arms of Ishtar, who laid her cheek against his breast, and wept for very joy because of his safe return.

'Where is the dove,' he asked, 'that flew before me through the tent-door even now?'

'There is no dove here but me,' said Ishtar tenderly. 'O Sarchedon, for you I would ever be the Bird of Love!'

He looked fondly down in those trustful pleading eyes. 'The Bird of Love,' he answered, 'and better, dearer still—the Bird of Peace!'

THE END.

LONDON: ROBSON AND SONS, PRINTERS, PANCRAS ROAD, N.W.

www.ingramcontent.com/pod-product-compliance
Lightning Source LLC
Chambersburg PA
CBHW021409230426
43666CB00006B/686